JN440089

조익제 변호사와 함께 영어로 읽는

Introduction to the US American Legal System

for Korean Speaking Lawyers and Law Students

미국법 입문

Vol. 2

The Law of Sales, Torts, Business Associations and Procedural Questions

매매법, 불법행위법, 회사법 및 절차법

2. EDITION

2009

written by

Dr. Alexander Dörrbecker, LL.M.

Attorney at Law *(New York)*

Dr. Oliver Rothe, LL.M.

Attorney at Law *(Germany)*

translated and additionally commented in Korean

by

Ikze Cho

Attorney at Law *(Germany)*

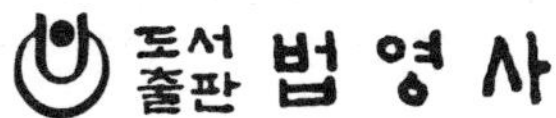

Dörrbecker, Dr. Alexander
Rothe, Dr. Oliver
Cho, Ikze

Introduction to the US American Legal System, Vol. 1
for Korean Speaking Lawyers and Law Students

2. Korean Language Edition 2009

ISBN 978-89-7032-254-4

Published by
BubYoungSa Publishing Co. and Lee International IP & Law Group

Preface

In this book we continue our introduction to the U.S. legal system. Again, the reader will find legal principles that are similar and those that are completely different from principles the Korean law student and lawyer is familiar with. This volume shall give again an overview over the areas of the U.S. legal system discussed.

This volume starts with an introduction to the law of sales. This area of law has some similarities to the Korean legal system. All cases applicable to it are governed by a legislative act, the Uniform Comercial Code (U.C.C.), and not by the common law principles. The founders of the U.C.C. even studied continental european civil codes before creating this new system of rules.

The following chapter will be the law of torts. Although this area of U.S. law is mainly based on common law principles the reader will be able to find many similar aspects of substantive law especially as far as the broad principles is concernd.

The area of business law is in part governed by the common law and in part by statutory law. Especially the law regulating corporations contains many aspects familiar to the Korean law student.

The final chapter deals with procedural questions. In this chapter the reader may realize that procedural law contains many problems the Korean procedural law does not know. Especially the differenciation between federal procedural law and state law lead to questions that are new to the Korean perspective.

The method, how we introduce the U.S. legal system to the reader, is the same as used in volume one. Again, you will find many summarized cases. As already stated in the preface to volume one this approach has two main advantages: Firstly, you can generally keep legal problems better in mind if you can think of concrete names and cases. Secondly, the cases will give you an insight in the way American lawyers think.

This volume also contains diagrams which sum up what we have explained in each previous part and they make it easier to keep in mind the material discussed.

Munster, Seoul, February 2009 Alexander Dorrbecker
Oliver Rothe
Ikze Cho
Attorneys at law

한국판에 붙이는 글

독자들의 호응에 힘입어 미국법 1권에 이어서 2권도 제2판을 출간하게 되었으며 방주 부분에만 약간의 수정을 가하였다. 곧이어 영국법 2권도 출간될 예정인데 이로써 영미법 시리즈가 완간이 된다.

본 시리즈를 통하여 "영어로 배우는 법학" "국제화 시대의 법학"의 필요성을 전달할 수만 있었다면 그것만으로도 보람된 일이라고 생각한다. 많은 학생들이 로스쿨을 졸업하고, 또한 외국의 로스쿨에서도 공부하여 풍부한 교양을 지닌 실력있는 법률가가 되기를 바란다. 저 역시 선생이 아니라 함께 배우는 학생의 입장에서 본 시리즈를 소개할 뿐이다. 많은 독자 의견을 통해서 더 유익한 책이 되어가면 더 바랄 것이 없을 것이다.

우리나라 대학은 이미 배우는 즐거움을 많이 잃어버리지 않았는가 생각이 든다.

서울대학교의 어느 교수께서는 학생의 70～80%가 족보로 공부를 한다며 대학이 "막장 대학"이 되어간다고 비판하셨다고 한다. 본서는 소위 "스펙"(specifications)을 갖추기 위한 수험서가 아니라 행복한 공부, 배우는 즐거움을 위하여 기획된 책이다. 할 수 있다면 대학생들이 많이 읽고 학구적인 대학생활을 해나가는데 도움을 삼았으면 좋겠다.

본서는 헌법과 계약법을 설명한 제1권과 동일한 방식을 사용하여 (영어본문, 한국어 단어 해설, 많은 도표), 매매법, 불법행위법, 회사법 그리고 절차법을 상세히 설명하고 있다. 독자들은 제2권에서도 쉽게 정리한 미국의 판례들을 접하게 될 것이다. 이미 제1권에서 밝힌 바와 같이 미국법의 이론과 판례는 미국어(영어)로 읽을 때에 가장 잘 이해할 수 있으며, 배우는 기쁨도 크리라 생각하는데, 본서는 이러한 목적에 잘 부합하는 책이라 생각한다.

본 시리즈에서 취급하는 분야는 미국법의 기본적인 분야들이므로, 미국 로스쿨의 시험과목일 뿐만 아니라, 국내의 대학, 대학원, 사법연수원 등에서도 이미 해당 분야의 강좌가 개설되어 있다. 따라서, 본 시리즈는 미국법 강의의 기본서 또는 참고서로 활용될 수 있으며, 이미 본서를 기본교재로 채용한 대학도 생겼다.

매매법과 회사법 등을 설명하는 본서가 국내 법학도 뿐만 아니라, 미국에 진출했거나, 진출하고자 하는 국내기업의 실무진들, 이를 지원하는 행정관료들, 미국을 이해하고자 하는 일반인들 및 미국을 무대로 활동하는 한인교포들에게도 좋은 길잡이가 되기를 바란다.

2009년 2월 20일

변호사(독일) 조 익 제

Contents

Chapter Four

Chapter Five

Chapter Six

Chapter Seven

Bibliography

Alces/Hansford	Sales, Leases and Bulk Transfers (1989)
Clark	Corporate Law (1986)
Crump e.a.	Cases and Materials on Civil Produce (4th ed., 2001)
Diamond e.a.	Understanding Torts (2nd ed.)
Gerber	Business Reorganizations (3rd ed.)
Green	Bassic Civil Procedure (1979)
Harper/James/Gray	The Law of Torts (1986)
Henn/Alexander	Handbook of the Law of Corporations and Other Business Enterprises (1983)
Hynes	Agency, Partnership and the LLC (6th ed., 1999)
Kane/Miller	Civil Procedure (1993)
King e.a.	Sales Law
Klein/Coffee	Business Organisation and Finance
Lawrence	Understanding Sales and Leases of Goods (1996)
Levmore	Foundations of Tort Law (1993)
McGovern/Lawrence	Contracts and Sales: Cases and Problems (1986)
Moore	Federal Practice (looseleaf)
Prosser/Keeton	On Torts (1984)
Rabin	Perspectives on Tort Law (1990)
Romano	Foundations of Coporate Law (1993)
Reuschlein/Gregory	The Law of Agency and Partnership (1990)
Ribstein/Mason/Letsou	Business Associations (3rd ed., 1996)
Shapo	Tort and Injury Law (2nd ed., 2000)
Shreve/Raven-Hansen	Understanding Civil Procedure (2nd ed., 1994)
Simon	The Anatomy of a Lawsuit (1996)
Vandall/Wertheimer	Tort: Cases and Problems (1997)
Vetri	Tort Law and Practice (1998)

Chapter Four

Sales

Part 1: Introduction

In Chapter Three we discussed the general law of contracts. The rules discussed there apply in most contractual situations. However, special rules haven been developed for contracts involving transactions in goods. 거래(재화가 오고 감)

A new uniform Act was drafted in 1951 by the Commissioners on Uniform State Laws, and this new Act now appears as Article 2 of the Uniform Commercial Code ("U.C.C."). 법률 / 통일상법전

We will talk about the following topics:

- formation (part 2)
- performance of the contract (part 3)
- remedies (part 4)
- warranties (part 5)

A. Subject Matter of Article 2

The law of Sales is applicable only to transactions involving "**goods**." 상품, 재화

I. Sale

A sale is a contract pursuant to whose terms goods are passed from the seller for a **consideration** called a **price**. [U.C.C. §2-106(l)].

II. Goods

"Goods" include all tangible chattels – basically **anything movable** at the time it is identified to the contract of sale. Excluded by this definition are transactions involving real property (but crops are included, see below); transactions in paper rights (e.g., promissory notes, stocks, or bonds); the 유형의 / 동산 / 수확, 곡물 / 약속어음 / 주식 / 유가증권

sale of services (e.g., a membership in a health spa); and the sale of intangibles (e.g., insurance). [U.C.C. §2-105(i)] 온천, 건강천 무형의 / 보험

III. "Goods" attached to realty

Article 2 does not apply to the sale of land itself or any interest therein. However, it does apply to the sale of certain kinds of property attached to land, if severed and sold apart from the land:

1. Crops

Growing crops, whether natural to the land itself or cultivated are within the scope of Article 2. 재배하다

2. Minerals

Minerals (e.g. timber to be cut), ice, or water, or any structure on the land, if to be severed by the seller, are covered by Article 2. If not, the contract is not subject to Article 2. 나무 매도인

3. Fixtures

Anything else attached to the land which can be removed without material harm thereto ("fixtures") is covered by Article 2, whether it is to be severed by the buyer, the seller, or some third person. [U.C.C. §2-107(l), (2)] 고정물, 정착물

4. Services

Although contracts to perform services are not transactions in goods, many courts apply Article 2 to such contracts, either on a Restatement of Contract basis or "by analogy" to Article 2. 유추적용에 의해

B. Definitions

I. Merchants

U.C.C. Article 2 draws distinctions between **merchants** and nonmerchants, and in certain cases, holds merchants to higher 상인

standards than those for nonmerchants. Under the U.C.C., a "merchant" is a party who:

- Regularly deals in **goods** of the kind sold; — 장사하다, 거래하다 / 매도한 것과 같은 종류의
- Otherwise holds himself out as having **special knowledge** or skill as to the practices or goods involved; or — 기능, 기술
- Employs an **agent** who fits within these categories. [U.C.C. §2-104(1)] — 대리인

II. Good Faith

First, and most important, every contract or duty within the scope of the U.C.C. imposes an **obligation of good faith** in its performance or enforcement. [U.C.C. §1-203] This obligation cannot be waived by the parties. [U.C.C. §1-102(3)] There are a number of court decisions holding that good faith is an absolute condition precedent to any protection by the other U.C.C. provisions. Hence, if a person's action is clearly in bad faith, that person cannot claim the benefits of the usual U.C.C. rules.

의무
이행 / 강제, 관철
포기하다
정리조건

Part 2: Formation

The requirements of **offer** and **acceptance** applicable to ordinary contracts are, of course, applicable to sales contracts. A sales contract need take no specific form. Under the U.C.C., the manner in which a contract is formed is not limited to an oral or a written agreement. Instead, the Code focuses on the element of agreement between the parties and provides that a sales contract can be formed in any manner sufficient to show an agreement, including conduct by both parties that recognizes the existence of such a contract. [U.C.C. §2-204(l)]

청약 / 승낙
통상적인, 일반적인
~에 집중하다
규정하다

A. Offer and Acceptance

I. Firm Offer

Pursuant to the U.C.C. "**firm**" offers are irrevocable, even without consideration, if they meet the following requirements:

구속력 있는

- The firm offer must be made **in connection with a contract to sell goods**, as the Code does not purport to revise the general body of contract law outside its scope; 언명하다 개정하다
- The firm offer must be made by a "**merchant**"; and 상인
- The offer must be in a signed writing and must state that it **will be held open** (although use of the words "firm offer" is probably enough).

If the above conditions are met, the offer is irrevocable ("firm") but the period of irrevocability may not exceed three months. 초과하다

No consideration is necessary to make the offer irrevocable as long as the offer gives words of firmness, is in writing, and is signed by the merchant. 구속, 구속성

Mid-South Packers, Inc. v. Shoney's, Inc. – 761 F.2d 1117 (1985)

The plaintiff and the defendant engaged in negotiations for defendant to purchase pork products from plaintiff. Eventually, the parties agreed that the plaintiff would sell to the defendant on an as-ordered basis. Part of the initial agreement was that there would be a 45-day notice of any price increase. Subsequently, when the defendant made an order, the plaintiff informed the defendant of a 10-cents-per-pound increase. The defendant protested, but purchased anyway. The defendant ordered from the plaintiff several more times. On the last order, the defendant deducted a $ 26,208 "offset" for what the defendant believed to be plaintiff's improper price increases. The plaintiff sued for breach, and the trial court granted it summary judgment. The defendant appealed. 협상 / 주문한 바와 같이 / 증가, 상승, 인상

Issue

In the absence of a requirements contract, does each sale of a product to a purchaser carry its own contractual terms? 없음, 부재 / 수요계약*, 공급계약

* 장기적인 물품 공급의 기초관계를 규정하는 지속적 계약

Holding and Reasoning

Yes. In the absence of a requirements contract, each sales of a product to a purchaser carries its own contractual terms. Unless a purchaser has agreed to buy all its requirements from a supplier, each sale order is a contract unto itself and carries its own terms. Here, there was no such requirement contract. Therefore, the clause stating that an increase in price would be made only after 45 days notice was, at most, a firm offer which expired when the first sale was made. Each sale thereafter was based on such terms as were negotiated then. Here, the plaintiff offered a sale at higher prices, and the defendant accepted. A contract was thus made, and the defendant was liable for the full price.

II. Medium of Acceptance

An offer may be accepted using the following methods: [U.C.C. §2-206(l)(a)]

1. Any Reasonable Manner

An offer is construed as inviting acceptance in any reasonable manner and by any medium reasonable under the circumstances.

해석하다

2. Acceptance by Shipment

An offer for prompt or current **shipment** is accepted either by a prompt promise to ship or by the act of shipment. [U.C.C. §2-206(1)(b)]

납품
납품하다

The U.C.C. also deals with the effect of shipping nonconforming goods. The shipment of nonconforming goods may be treated either as an acceptance or as a counteroffer, depending on Seller's actions in conjunction therewith.

합의하지 아니한, 합의한 것과 일치하지 않는 / 반대청약
관련하여(with)

III. Acceptance by Performance

Commencement of the performance specified in the offer constitutes acceptance of the offer, provided that the offeree-acceptor notifies the offeror within a reasonable time that

시작, 개시함

performance has commenced. [U.C.C. §2-206(2)] 이행

IV. Battle of the Forms

Adopting the premise that both parties are relying on the existence of a contract despite their **clashing forms**, the U.C.C. establishes a general rule that a contract can be formed under such circumstances, unless the responding offeree specifically states that there shall be no contract unless the original offeror expressly accepts the second set of terms. If the offeree specifically limits the contract to these new terms, the response is treated merely as a counteroffer, and no contract has been created (until the offeror accepts). [U.C.C. §2-207(l)]

의존하다, 믿다
대립하다
답변하다, 응답하다
단지 / 반대청약

The new terms are **construed as mere proposed additions to the contract**; i.e., they do not become part of the contract. These new terms must be separately accepted to modify the original offer. If the new terms would materially alter the original terms, the new terms are automatically stricken and do not become part of the contract. [U.C.C. §2-207(2)(b)]

해석하다
배제하다

Roto-Lith, Ltd. v. F.P. Bartlett & Co. – 297 F.2d 497 (1962)

The plaintiff manufactures plastic bags which are sealed by means of an emulsion sold by the defendant. The plaintiff bought emulsion from the defendant that failed to adhere, and so the plaintiff brought an action for breach of contract. The standard acceptance form generated by defendant in response to plaintiff's order had an express disclaimer of any warranty whatsoever on the reverse0 side. The defendant sent acceptance to the plaintiff.

생산하다
계약위반

The plaintiff claims that under the U.C.C. §2-207, the defendant was bound to the terms of plaintiff's order, and that the warranty disclaimer on the back of the acceptance letter was a proposal for additional conditions that the plaintiff did not accept.

보증책임의 배제

Issue

To what extent may a buyer ignore additional or changed terms in a reply from an seller that does not mirror the original terms proposed by the buyer, and still result in contract formation?

Holding and Reasoning

A response by a seller that states additional terms or conditions that materially alter the obligation solely to the disadvantage of the buyer is an acceptance that is expressly conditional on assent to the additional terms.

추가조건

수락

It is unrealistic to assume that when the seller adds the additional terms it wishes to be bound to all the terms that the buyer set forth, and rely solely on the good nature of the buyer as to whether he would accept the additional terms. The court also reasoned [perhaps erroneously] that since the plaintiff accepted delivery of the goods, he had become bound to the terms set forth by the defendant.

전제하다, 받아들이다

B. Defenses

I. ***Statute of Frauds***

형식요건

The U.C.C. Statute of Frauds applies only to contracts for the sale of goods having a price of $500 or more. [U.C.C. §2-201] A sales contract that does not comply with the Statute of Frauds is **unenforceable** – i.e., neither party can force the other to proceed therewith. However, the contract is not void; if the parties choose to perform, enforceable rights may be created.

상품매매

강제, 관철할 수 없는

1. Writing

One method of satisfying the Statute of Frauds, and thus rendering the contract enforceable, is the **production of a written note** or memorandum signed by the party to be charged. [U.C.C. §2-201(l)]

충족하다

문서를 작성하다

의무를 부담하는

The writing is sufficient if it indicates that a contract for sale has been made and specifies the quantity term. The

Code drafters felt that quantity is the one term that is impossible to imply by law. [U.C.C. §2-201(l)] 법의 입안자

It is essential that the memorandum be signed by the party to be charged. **No particular form** of signature is required (it may be typed, stamped, etc.), and it need not appear at the bottom of the writing. 요구하다

2. Confirmatory Memo Rule

In **contracts between merchants**, if one party, within a reasonable time after an oral agreement has been made sends to the other party a written confirmation of the understanding sufficient under the Statute of Frauds to bind the sender, it will also bind the recipient if he has reason to know of the confirmation's consent; and he does not object to it within 10 days of receipt [U.C.C. §2-201(2)]. 구두의 / 확인 / 이의를 제기하다

II. Unconscionability 미풍양속에 반함

Unconscionability is determined on a case-by-case basis. The test is whether, at the time of execution, the contract or one of its provisions could result in unfair surprise and was oppressive to a disadvantaged party. 사안별로 / 놀람 / 과도한 부담을 지우는

III. Statute of Limitations 시효

The U.C.C. creates a **four-year statute of limitations** on actions to enforce rights or obligations under any contract sale, oral or written. [U.C.C. §2-725(1)] 의무

C. Parol Evidence Rule

In a sales contract, the U.C.C. rejects the assumption that because a writing has been worked out which is final on some matters, it is to be taken as including all matters agreed upon. Instead, before the writing can operate to exclude parol evidence, the court must specifically find that the **parties intended the writing to be the complete** and exclusive statement of the terms of the agreement. [U.C.C. §2-202(b)] 추정, 전제 / 기능하다, 역할을 하다 / 계약조건

If the court does not find that the writing was intended to be a complete and exclusive statement of the terms, it may receive parol evidence of consistent, additional terms (i.e., terms not expressly or impliedly contained in the writing). 의도하다

A term is not a consistent, additional term (and is therefore barred by the parol evidence rule) if it is the sort of thing that if true would certainly already be in the writing. However, if it is the sort of thing that might naturally be left out of the writing, it is a consistent, additional term and may be admitted. [U.C.C. §2-202] 일관성있는 배제하다

D. Terms of the Contract

Eastern Air Lines, Inc. v. Gulf Oil Corp. – 415 F. Supp. 429 (S.D. Fla. 1975)

Plaintiff and defendant had been dealing for several years in good faith. The defendant had supplied jet fuel to the plaintiff based on a requirements contract for all the fuel they would reasonably need at a price based on the fluctuating Texas Sour index (a measure of the market price). However, when OPEC raised prices during the oil embargo, the Texas Sour index became much lower than the real world market price because it only reported domestic oil prices which were under government control. Because of this, the defendant threatened to cut off plaintiff's fuel supply if the plaintiff did not agree to pay a higher price than stipulated in the requirements contract. The plaintiff obtained a temporary injunction and sued for specific performance of the contract. The defendant argued that the contract was invalid because 1) it lacked mutuality of obligation, and 2) the plaintiff breached the contract by practicing "fuel freighting" whereby a plane bought more fuel than it needed from the lowest price gas station, and then only "topped off" at the higher priced station.

선의 / 비행기 연료
합리적으로 / 변하다
석유금수조치
내국의, 국내의
공급
확정하다
가처분
계약이행 청구소송을 제기하다
상호연관성

Issue

1. Is there sufficient consideration for a contract even though the plaintiff had no obligation to buy a particular

amount (quantity was not fixed)?

2. Was there a breach of contract by plainitff's practice of "fuel freighting", even though it was common practice and known by the defendant?

Holding and Reasoning

1. Yes. A requirements contract is binding on the seller to provide a reasonable amount of product to the buyer, consistent with commercial standards of fair dealing, and is binding on the buyer to act in good faith in making orders consistent with his requirements. 공급계약, 수요계약

1. Using U.C.C. §2-306, both parties identified and understood the risks involved in making the requirements contract. The fact that the price went up drastically was one of the foreseeable risks that was redistributed to the defendant when the plaintiff and the defendant redistributed their respective pre-contractual risks. Since the parties had relied upon each other over the years in light of the understanding of these risks, it should not have been a surprise to the defendant that he was contractually bound. 예측가능한 / 부담시키다

2. No. A requirements contract is not breached by the buyer making fluctuations in the requirements in accordance with normal business practices of which the seller is aware. 변화

The practice of "fuel freighting" in the industry was a well known and accepted practice, and as such did not violate the nature of the requirements contract which required good faith dealing. "Good-faith" between merchants means "honesty in fact and the observance of reasonable commercial standards of fair dealing in the trade." The court then awarded specific performance because to award anything less would be useless. 정직 준수

E. Modification

Skinner v. Tober Foreign Motors, Inc. – 345 Mass. 429, 187 N.E.2d 669 (1963)

The plaintiff purchased a plane from the the defendant with an installment contract to pay $200/mo. The plane then immediately had engine troubles which required the 할부

replacement of the engine for $1,400. The plaintiff was unable to make the payments and pay for the repair, so he offered to return the plane as-is, in return for a cancellation of the previous agreement. After some negotiation, the parties arranged orally to reduce the payments to $100/Mo., for the first year. After a few months, the defendant decided that the payments were too small, and he repossessed the plane. The plaintiff sued for the amount he had paid.

대체

구두로

Issue

Is the oral agreement to lessen the payments to $100/Mo. binding, even though it was "without consideration"?

감소, 경감하다

Holding and Reasoning

Yes. U.C.C. §2-209 states that an "agreement modifying a contract...needs no consideration to be binding."

변경하다

The court reasoned that the oral arrangement was binding, even though the plaintiff did not have to do as much as they were originally obligated to do. The dealer was free to contract with reference to the risk that the buyer would default on the installment contract.

~에 관하여

Diagram 1

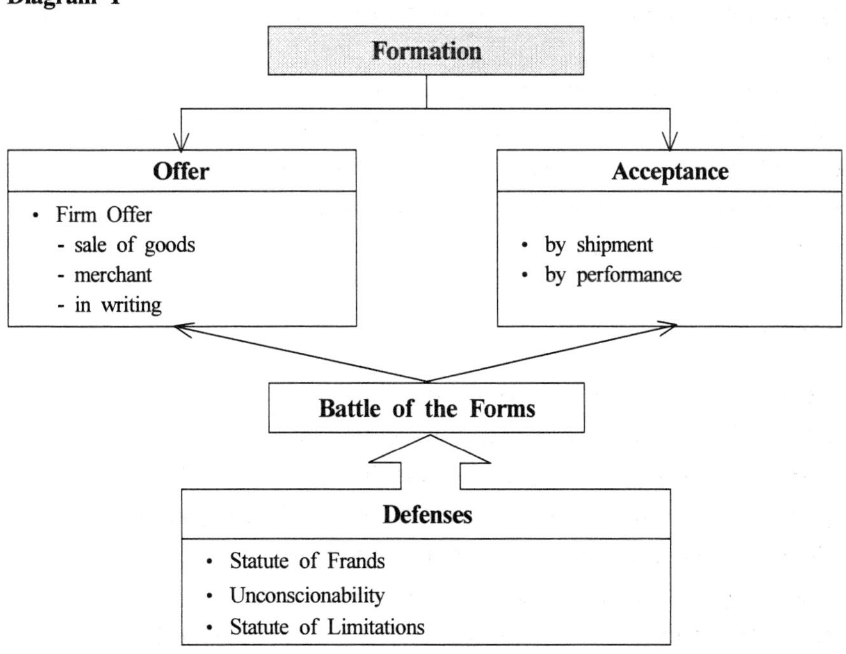

Part 3: Performance of the Contract

Performance of a sales contract generally means that the seller **delivers the goods** to the buyer, who accepts and pays for them. 납품하다, 공급하다

A. Performance by Seller

I. Shipment by Seller

A shipment contract is one that **requires the seller to deliver the goods to a carrier** at the place of shipment, after which, the seller's responsibility with respect to the goods ceases. The U.C.C. establishes a basic presumption that all contracts are shipment contracts unless the parties expressly agree to the contrary. [U.C.C. §2-503] 운송계약, 선적계약 / 운송업자 / 전제

Besides delivering the goods to the carrier, the U.C.C. requires the seller to make a contract with the carrier on behalf of the buyer as may be reasonable, considering the nature of the goods and the other circumstances of the case. [U.C.C. §2-504(a)] ~대신

Commercial contracts are often made in abbreviated terms indicated by mercantile symbols. This is particularly true in the area of shipment, where particular terms – **F.O.B.** ("free on board"), **F.A.S.** ("free alongside"), or **C.I.F.** ("cost, insurance, and freight") – are widely used by those in business to indicate whether they intend a particular contract to be a shipment contract or a destination contract. 상인간의 계약 / 축약된 조건 / 상업계의

II. Noncarrier Cases

In cases where delivery is to be made directly to the buyer by the seller without the need for carrier transportation, the **seller must offer ("tender") the goods to the buyer** to discharge the seller's duties under the sales contract. Of course, the seller need not make actual delivery where the buyer is unwilling to take the goods; the seller need only tender the goods, not force them on the buyer. 제공하다 / (책임을) 벗다 / 강제하다

Tender of delivery must be made at a reasonable hour [U.C.C. §2-503(1)(a)]. The place where delivery is to be made – in the absence of contrary agreement – is the seller's (not the buyer's) place of business or residence. [U.C.C. §2-308] 사업지 / 주소

III. Repudiation

Oloffson v. Coomer – 296 N.E.2d 871 (1973)

Oloffson (buyer) was a grain dealer. Coomer (seller) was a farmer. Buyer and seller contracted for the purchase of 40,000 bushels of corn to be delivered half in October, and half in December. The contract price was $1.12 per bushel. In June, the seller notified the buyer that he did not intend to plant the corn, at which time the price was $1.16/bushel. The buyer insisted that he perform, and waited until just before the time scheduled for delivery to effect cover. However, in the mean time, the price of corn skyrocketed, and the cover price was $1.49/bushel.

곡물 중개인
부쉘(약, 35리터)
통지하다
(~을) 심다
주장하다
하늘로 치솟다

Issue

How long may a buyer wait to effect cover when a seller repudiates before performance? 거절하다

Holding and Reasoning

A commercially reasonable time.

The court followed the remedy options in U.C.C. §2-610 for anticipatory repudiation. The court reasoned that a commercially reasonable time could be less than the time for performance, particularly when the notice of repudiation is unconditional and clear. Furthermore, the court found that the buyer acted in bad faith by failing to notify the seller of the usage of trade of letting his customers out of the contract at any time if they paid the contract- market differential on the date of repudiation. In bad faith, the buyer took advantage of the seller's lack of knowledge, thinking that he could continue to wait before covering. Thus, when the buyer learned of the breach, the commercially reasonable time expired, and the buyer then had a right to pursue damages

미리 행한 거절
상관습 / 고객
추구하다, ~을 얻으려 하다

under U.C.C. §2-713. In this case, the contract- market differential on the day the buyer learned of the repudiation.

B. Performance by Buyer

The buyer's first duty is to furnish facilities reasonably suited for receipt of the goods. [U.C.C. §2-503(l)(b)]

제공하다
수령

I. Acceptance and Payment of Goods

The buyer's basic duty is to **"accept and pay for"** the goods. [U.C.C. §2-301]

1. Acceptance

Acceptance may occur by words or conduct of the buyer signifying approval of the goods delivered.

발생하다
동의

Once the buyer accepts the goods, payment is due at the contract rate. The buyer cannot thereafter reject the goods as nonconforming. [U.C.C. §2-607(l)(2)]

계약조건
(계약에) 부합하지 않는

2. Payment

The second part of the buyer's basic duty under any sales contract is to pay for the goods. [U.C.C. §2-301]

Unless credit has been arranged, the buyer must tender payment as a condition concurrent to the seller's obligation to tender delivery of the goods to the buyer. **Payment is due at the time of delivery**. [U.C.C. §2-310]

대출
납기일

Payment is sufficient when made in any manner reasonable in the ordinary course of business, unless the seller demands payment in legal tender and gives the buyer an extension of time necessary to procure the legal tender. This means that, in the usual case, payment by check is sufficient. [U.C.C. §2-511(3)]

통상적인 사업의 흐름, 경과
연장

Payment normally is in money, but this is not essential. The parties can agree on any form of consideration.

II. Right of Inspection

Unless the parties agree otherwise, the buyer has the **<u>right to inspect</u>** the goods before payment or acceptance. [U.C.C. §2-513(l)] 조사권

1. Exercising Right of Inspection

Inspection must be made **within a reasonable time** after receipt of the goods, or the right is lost. What is reasonable depends on all of the circumstances of the transaction, including the nature of the goods, <u>marketability</u>, usage of trade, and the like. Inspection must be made at a reasonable hour. [U.C.C. §2-513(1)] 시장성

Under the U.C.C., the buyer is permitted to make the inspection at any reasonable place. [U.C.C. §2-513(l)]

If <u>visual inspection</u> is not sufficient to determine whether the goods conform, the buyer has the **right to test a reasonable amount of the goods**, and to use and consume the same in such tests, as long as these actions are reasonable. [U.C.C. §2-513(1)] 시각적 조사

2. Rejection

If the goods that the seller delivers do not conform to the contract, the buyer is <u>entitled</u> to reject them if the buyer follows certain formalities. [U.C.C. §2-6011] 권리가 있는

Diagram 2

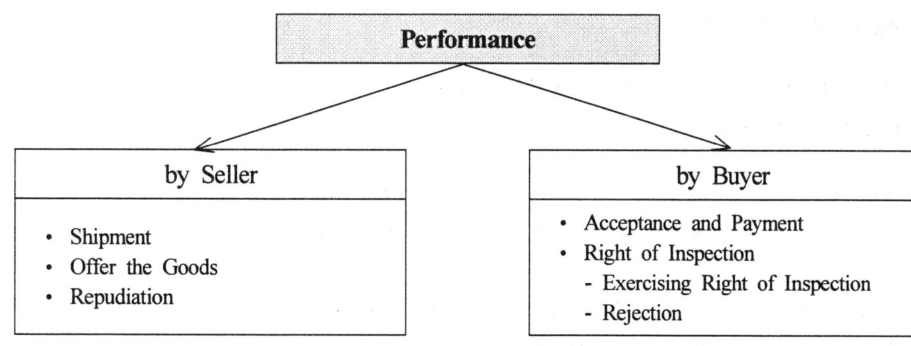

Part 4: Remedies

Whenever a breach occurs, either the buyer or the seller (whoever is the aggrieved party) will take remedial action. Therefore, whenever your question involves a breach of contract, you need to consider the remedies available to the injured party.

A. Seller's Prelitigation Remedies

Various remedies are provided under the U.C.C. to protect a seller who, although under an obligation to deliver goods to the buyer, has either not been paid or has good reason to believe that there will be no payment.

I. Right to Withhold Delivery or Demand Cash Payment

At common law (and under the Sales Act), the seller was deemed to have an **implied-in-law "lien"** on the goods as security for the unpaid purchase price. The U.C.C. abandons any such notion, and instead simply provides that, under appropriate circumstances, a seller is entitled to withhold delivery of the goods [U.C.C. §2-703(a)] or demand cash payment for them notwithstanding an earlier agreement for credit [U.C.C. §2-702(l)].

질권, 담보권
담보 / 포기하다

II. Reclamation of Goods

The U.C.C. recognizes an unpaid seller's right to reclaim goods in two situations:

미지불의 / 반환청구하다

- ***cash sales*** where the buyer pays by check at the time of delivery, but the check is returned for insufficient funds [U.C.C. §2-507(2)]; and
- ***credit sales*** where, after delivery of the goods to the buyer, the seller discovers that the buyer is insolvent [U.C.C. §2-702(2)]. In the credit sale situation, the seller may reclaim the goods by demanding their return within 10 days after the buyer receives them. [U.C.C. §2-702(2)]

요구하다
수령하다

III. Stoppage in Transit

Once the goods have been delivered to a carrier for shipment, to the buyer, the unpaid seller cannot withhold delivery. However, a seller in such a position may have the right to stop the goods while they are in transit and resume possession thereof. This puts the seller back in the position he was in before the goods were delivered to the carrier, i.e., having the right to withhold delivery, to demand payment, etc.

운송인
유보하다
점유를 재개하다, 다시 점유하게 되다

IV. Identifying Conforming Goods

As shall be seen, the seller's primary **prelitigation remedy is to resell the goods.** However, before the seller can do so, the goods must be "identified" to the contract. Recall that identification consists either of contracting with reference to specific goods (e.g., "this horse") or of designating (by the seller's action) certain goods as being those to be delivered in performance of the contract. [U.C.C. §2-501(l)] If the buyer breaches and the seller still has possession of conforming goods not yet identified to the contract or goods in the process of manufacture, what should the seller do?

되팔다, 재판매하다
지정하다, 특정하다

V. Resale

The most logical thing for a seller to do when in possession of goods that the buyer has refused to accept is to resell them and then **sue the buyer for any loss sustained by the seller on the resale.** The U.C.C. recognizes this course of action and expressly provides that where the seller resells the goods, the seller may recover as damages the difference between the resale price and the contract price (less any expenses saved in consequence of the buyer's breach). Of course, the resale must be made in good faith and in a commercially reasonable manner. [U.C.C. §2-706(1)]

제소이유, 청구이유
재판매가격 / 계약가격
선의
경제적으로 합리적인 방식

VI. Cancellation

The final prelitigation remedy afforded the seller by the U.C.C. is to "cancel" the contract [U.C.C. §2-703(f)], cancel-

취소, 철회하다

lation being defined as putting "an end to the contract for reason of breach" [U.C.C. §2-106(4)].

B. Buyer's Prelitigation Remedies

I. Sale of Goods to Recover

If the buyer has paid the full or part of the purchase price and has received goods that do not conform to the contract he is in a position substantially similar to that of an unpaid seller still in possession of goods. Therefore, the U.C.C. gives the buyer a **security interest in the goods** for the amount of the prepayment, and provides that if the buyer appropriately offers to restore the seller's goods and demands repayment of the price paid, and the seller then refuses, the buyer may sell the goods. [U.C.C. §2-711(3)]

매매가, 매매가격

담보권

II. Cover

The most important remedy afforded to a buyer by the U.C.C. is the right to "cover" – **to go out into the market and purchase substitute goods.** As long as the buyer acts reasonably, the buyer can then sue the seller for any excess of the cover price over the contract price. [U.C.C. §2-712(1)]

대체물

대체가격

Panhandle Agri-Service Inc. v. Becker – 644 P.2d 413 (1982)

Becker made a contract to sell Panhandle 10,000 tons of hay for $45/ton. When he still had 912 tons left to deliver, the market price had risen to $62/ton at the time and place of delivery, and Becker refused to sell. Panhandle sued for breach, and the trial court awarded it the difference between the $67/ton market price in Texas (where Panhandle had a contract to resell it) and the contract price of $45/ton, minus the cost of transportation from Kansas to Texas.

판매를 거부하다

(배상금을) 인정하다

Issue

What is the proper measure of damages for seller's breach in a standard sale of goods contract under the U.C.C.?

Holding and Reasoning

The difference between the market price at the time that the buyer learned of the breach and the contract price, together with any incidental and consequential damages, but less expenses saved in consequence of the seller's breach. 비용, 지출, 경비

First, the court reasoned that deducting the transportation cost was error because it was not money saved by Panhandle because of the breach. If Panhandle were to cover, then it would have had to pay for the transportation anyway, so it did not save. Then the court stated that since Panhandle decided NOT to cover, it was not entitled to consequential damages including lost profits. The buyer has the choice of covering and taking the actual damages including lost profits (the difference between what he would have made on resale if he had paid the contract price and the amount he actually did make from the substitute goods) or not covering, and making the difference between the market price and the contract price.

일실이익(逸失利益)
실제(로 발생한) 손해

III. Recoupment

The U.C.C. accords the buyer the right to deduct from payments to the seller any damages incurred through a nonconformity in the seller's performance under the particular contract. [U.C.C. §2-717] Thus, if the seller's deliveries are **short quantity or too late**, are freight collect when they should have been freight prepaid, or the buyer is damaged in any other way by the seller's breach, the buyer may deduct damages from the contract price.

(권리 등을) 인정하다, 주다
불일치
운임 후지급(= freight forward)
운임 선지급

C. Seller's Litigation Remedies

I. Action for Full Purchase Price

At common law, the seller of goods was not allowed to sue for specific performance. Why not? Because, from the seller's point of view, specific performance is actually a forced sale, and since the buyer is paying money, the courts deemed this sort of thing an action at law for damages.

약정채무의 이행, 계약이행
간주하다

Unlike the common law, the U.C.C. gives the seller a specific performance remedy, calling it an "action for the price," but limits the availability to three circumstances:

1. Technical "Acceptance" by Buyer

If the buyer has made an "acceptance" of the goods, the buyer must pay for the goods. [U.C.C. §2-709(l)(a)]

2. Passage to Buyer of Risk of Loss

If the goods are harmed or destroyed after the **risk of loss has passed** to the buyer, the buyer must pay the full purchase price. [U.C.C. §2-709(l)(a)] 손상된 / 파괴된

3. "White elephant?" goods

Where the goods still in the seller's possession are such that they cannot be resold, an action for the full price is allowed. This covers goods manufactured specially to order (eg., imprinted calendars), and goods for which there is no market other than the buyer. Under such circumstances, if the goods have been identified (designated) to the contract, and the seller after reasonable efforts has been unable to resell them or it is clear such efforts would be unavailing, the seller can sue the buyer for the full price. [U.C.C. §2-709(1)(b)]

점유 / 특별주문 생산품 / 노력

II. Action for Damages for Nonacceptance

Under the U.C.C., there are three measures of damages available to the seller when the buyer has refused to accept the goods: 방법, 수단, 조치

- the difference between the **contract and resale prices,**
- the difference between the **contract and market prices,** and
- **lost profits.**

1. Contract-Resale Differential

As noted, the U.C.C. presumes that the most logical and commercially reasonable action for the seller to take when the buyer refuses to accept goods is to resell them. If the seller does so in accordance with the U.C.C. provision on resale, the seller may recover the difference between the resale price and the contract price. [U.C.C. §2-706(l)]

재판매하다, (다른 이에게) 팔다
~에 따라

2. Contract-market Differential

Alternatively, the seller may recover against the buyer the difference between the contract price and the market price at the time and place that the goods were tendered. [U.C.C. §2-708(l)]

제공하다, 청약하다

3. Lost Profits

U.C.C. also sanctions a lost profits recovery where damages measured by either a contract-resale or contract-market differential formula are "inadequate to put the seller in as good a position as performance would have done." [U.C.C. §2-708(2)] Indeed, in many cases, this measure of damages turns out to be the most realistic one for the seller.

일실(逸失)이익

Neri v. Retail Marine Corp. – 285 N.E.2d 311 (1972)

Neri contracted to buy a boat from Retail Marine, a retail boat dealer who sold custom order boats. Neri placed a down payment of $4,250, but then became ill, and decided not to go through with the boat sale. By the time he notified the dealer of the repudiation, the boat had been manufactured and delivered to the dealer. The dealer resold the boat a few months later for the same price, but incurred $674 in incidental storage and maintenance fees. The dealer would have made $2,579 profit on the sale to Neri. Neri sued for the balance of his down payment, and the dealer countersued for the lost profit and incidental damages, claiming that he was injured by the breach even though he resold the boat for the same amount because he was only able to make one sale, where he should have realized the profit on two sales.

보트 소매상
주문생산 보트 / 계약금
거절
부수적인 / 보관(창고) 및 유지비
청산, 지불, (여기서는)계약금의 반환 / 반소를 제기하다, 맞고소하다

Issue

What is the measure of damages upon a buyer's breach

where the retail seller has a virtually unlimited supply of the goods?

재고, 공급

Holding and Reasoning

Under U.C.C. §2-708, if the contract-market differential does not put the seller in as good a position as he would have been if the buyer had performed, he may recover the profit he would have made had the buyer fully performed, together with any incidental damages.

부수적, 부차적인 손해

The court reasoned that there must be an offset in awards to protect the interests of both parties. Under U.C.C. §2-718, the buyer was entitled to a refund in any amount which exceeded fair liquidated damages, or absent a liquidated damage clause, any amount which exceeded lesser of 20% or $500. However, this buyer's right to restitution is subject to offset to the extent that liquidated damages would fail to put the seller in as good a position as he would have been if the seller performed. Even though the seller resold the boat at the market price, since he was not a private individual with only one boat to sell, but rather a dealer in the retailing of boats, he was actually permanently injured by having his number of sales forever reduced by one. Thus, the measure of damages should be that found in U.C.C. §2-708 because the contract－market difference was an inadequate remedy for a retailer. Thus, Neri was awarded restitution in the amount of $4,250 (the down payment) less $3,253 (the sum of the retailer's lost profit and incidental storage costs.)

변상, 상쇄

합의 위약금

초과하다

다치다, 상해를 입다

부적절한, 상당하지 않은

배상, 보상, 전보

D. Buyer's Litigation Remedies

I. Possessory Actions

1. Replevin

The U.C.C. authorizes the buyer to seek replevin (i.e., an **action to recover the goods**) if the goods are identified to the contract, and if after a reasonable effort, the buyer is unable to procure substitute goods (cover) in the market, or the circumstances reasonably indicate that such effort will be

반환청구소송

대체하다

unavailing. [U.C.C. §2-716(3)] (노력 등의) 효과가 없는, 무익한

2. Specific Performance

The U.C.C. permits specific performance in any case where goods are unique or in other proper circumstances. [U.C.C. §2-716(l)] 계약이행

II. Action for Damages for Nondelivery

Under the U.C.C., there are several measures of damages available to the buyer when the seller fails to deliver the goods contracted for. 납품하지 않다, 못하다

1. Contract-cover Differential

As noted, the U.C.C. presumes that the most logical and commercially reasonable thing for the buyer to do when the seller fails to deliver goods is to go into the market and purchase substitute goods, i.e., "cover." If the buyer does so, the buyer may recover the difference between the cover price and the contract price—as long as the **cover was chosen in good faith.** [U.C.C. §2-712(2)] 전제하다 / 구매하다 / 대체상품

2. Contract-market Differential

Alternatively, the buyer may recover against the seller the difference between the contract price and the market price at the time the buyer learned of the breach. [U.C.C. §2-713(1)] 계약가격 / 시장가격

3. Consequential Damages

In addition to the "contract-cover" or "contract-market" differential, the U.C.C. permits the buyer to recover for any **loss resulting from general or particular requirements and needs** of which the seller at the time of contracting had reason to know and which could not reasonably be prevented by cover or otherwise. [U.C.C. §2- 715(2)(a)] 요구사항

4. Incidental Damages

In addition, the buyer is entitled to recover any incidental 부수적인(부수적으로 발생한)

damages resulting from the seller's failure to deliver conforming goods. These damages include expenses reasonably incurred in inspection, receipt, transportation, care, and custody of goods rightfully rejected; any commercially reasonable charges in connection with effecting cover; and any other reasonable expense incident to the delay or other breach. [U.C.C. §2-715(1)]

손해 / 계약조건에 합치하는 제품 / 발생하다
수령
비용

5. Deduction for Expenses Saved

From any recovery received by the buyer, there must be deducted any expenses saved in consequence of the seller's breach (e.g., savings on cover must be deducted from any claimed incidental damages). [U.C.C. §§2-712(2), 2-713(1)]

E. Limitation of Remedies

Many times a sales contract of a small object costing a few pennies or a few dollars can involve huge consequential damages in the event of breach (e.g., airplane factory shut down by seller's refusal to deliver critical parts). Similarly, a buyer's failure to perform may cause substantial lost profits or other large consequential damages to the seller. For these reasons, **parties to sales contracts may seek to stipulate as to their ultimate liability by special provisions in their contract.**

포함하다, 포괄하다
(명문으로) 규정하다

1. Liquidated Damages Provision

The U.C.C. sets forth a new set of standards for determining the validity of liquidated damages clauses in sales contracts:

유효성 / 위약금 조항

First, the amount of damages pre-established to be paid in the event of default or breach by one or both parties must be reasonable. "**Reasonableness**" is measured in light of

- the anticipated or actual harm caused by the breach,
- the difficulties of proof of loss, and
- the inconvenience or nonfeasibility of otherwise obtaining an adequate remedy. [U.C.C. §2-718(1)]

예측되어진, 예상한
불편함 / 실행불가능

Second, if the sales contract fixes unreasonably large or small liquidated damages, the clause is void as a penalty. [U.C.C. §2-718(1)] 무효의

II. Limitations on Damages

The U.C.C. specifically permits the parties to limit or alter the measure of damages otherwise recoverable under the Code. Specific examples of permissible limitations include clauses restricting the buyer to a return of the goods and repayment of the price, or to repair and replacement of nonconforming goods and parts. [U.C.C. §2-719(1)(a)] 변경하다

III. "Exclusive Remedy" Provision

The parties are given broad latitude under the U.C.C. in **choosing their own remedies**, as long as minimum adequate remedies are available. If the contract provides for its own remedies in the event of default, resort to those remedies is optional with the aggrieved party unless the contract declares the remedy to be "exclusive," in which case it is the sole remedy. [U.C.C. §2-719(b)] (재량의) 폭 / 이행지체 /호소, (어떤 수단에) 호소하기

Diagram 3

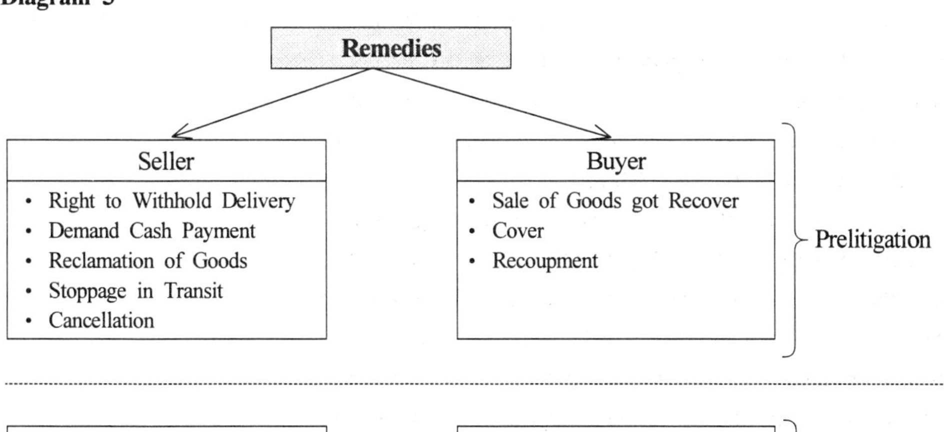

Part 5: Warranties

The concept of implied warranties has been embodied in the Code. Also, the Code divides warranties into two broad categories: **warranties of title** and **warranties of quality**, and first it is necessary to consider the warranty of title.

보증
법률하자에 관한 보증 / 품질에 관한 보증

A. Warranty of Title

The U.C.C. provides an **automatic warranty** that the seller will convey good title to the goods and that the transfer is rightful. The seller also warrants that the goods transfer is rightful. [U.C.C. §2-312] and that they will be delivered free of any claim of the seller's creditors of which the buyer has no knowledge. [U.C.C. §2-312(1)(b)]

양도하다, 이전하다 / 하자 없는 권리, 권원, 우량권원 / 적법한 / 보증하다
청구권 / 채권자

B. Express Warranties

I. Statement of Fact or Promise

1. Form of warranty

A statement of fact or promise made by the seller to the buyer in the course of negotiations that relates to the goods and is "part of the basis of the bargain" creates an express warranty that the goods will conform to the statement or promise made. [U.C.C. §2-313(l)(a)]

사실의 선언, 확정 / 약속

Contrary to the early common law rule, **no magic words** of warranty need be used. Any promise made in connection with the sale ("If it doesn't work, I'll fix it"), **description** of the goods ("When it arrives, it will be painted orange"), or **sample or model** ("It will look just like this baby over here") may be sufficient. It is not necessary that the seller use technical words such as "warranty" or "guarantee." [U.C.C. §2-313(l), (2)]

보증 / 보증계약*

In general, an express warranty may be written or oral. In

* warranty는 계약의 목적물이 주계약의 내용에 합치함을 명시적, 묵시적으로 보증하는 것이고, guarantee는 주계약의 유무를 물론하고 특정한 내용을 별도의 계약으로 보증하는 경우이다.

appropriate cases, it may be expressed by conduct, rather than words.

2. Seller's Intent or Culpability Immaterial

No intent to warrant is required. If the words used amount to a warranty, it is immaterial that the seller did not intend them as such or did not intend to be bound thereby. Liability is predicated on breach of contract, not fraud or negligence. Where the warranty is breached, the seller becomes absolutely liable. The fact that the warranty was given in good faith, or that the seller was innocent or nonnegligent in causing the breach, is immaterial. [U.C.C. §2-313(2)]

근거를 두다, 입각하다 / 기만, 기망 / 과실, 부주의
전적인 책임을 지는
비본질적인(주의, "비물질적인" 아님)

II. Basis of the Bargain

Under the U.C.C., not only must the alleged warranty "relate to the goods" (an obvious enough requirement), but it also must go to the "**basis of the bargain**." [U.C.C. §2-313 (l)] What does this mean? It means that the statement must have been part of the deal; it must have been the sort of thing that played some part in the buyer's decision to buy.

거래, 법률행위

1. Time of Warranting

Under the U.C.C., however, if a post-transactional affirmation in fact becomes part of the "basis of the bargain," it can be deemed a modification of the contract, and will be effective even without any new consideration. [U.C.C. §2-209]

계약이후의 확인
간주하다

2. Unread Warranties

If the seller makes an express warranty but the buyer does not learn of it until after the sale (e.g., the buyer sees an old advertisement), can the buyer recover for breach of the warranty? The technical argument against this is that the **unread warranty can hardly be "part of the basis of the bargain."** However, the buyer might prevail by claiming to be a third party beneficiary of the express warranty made to those who did see the warranty and purchased as a result of it. Such parties would legitimately expect any purchaser hurt

승소하다, 이기다

by breach of the warranty to be able to sue the warrantor for the breach. 보증을 하는 자, 보증인

C. Implied Warranties

In addition to any express warranties that may be made in connection with the sale by some statement or act of the seller, the law may imply certain other warranties simply because a sale of goods has been consummated. These are the implied warranties, which are created by law to promote higher standards and to discourage sharp dealings in business. They are imposed irrespective of the seller's intentions, and despite the fact that the seller has made no representations or promises whatsoever concerning the goods. Unless expressly negated by the parties or the circumstances, they arise by operation of law in every sale of goods, new or used, as part of the seller's cost of doing business.

완성하다
장려하다, 진흥하다
곤란하게 하다, 낙담시키다 / (의견이 일치하지 않는) 대립된 매매, 거래,

I. Warranty of Merchantability

In every mercantile contract of sale where it is not expressly disclaimed, the law implies a warranty that the **goods shall be of "merchantable" quality.** [U.C.C. §2-314]

상계약, 상인간의 계약
배제하다
"상거래가 가능한"

The U.C.C. imposes the implied warranty of merchantability only upon a seller who is a "merchant with respect to goods of that kind." [U.C.C. §2-314(l)]

The U.C.C. establishes a six-part definition of merchantability. Goods must meet at least all six standards (and any others the courts add to the merchantability definition). The standards are:

상거래(가능)성

- The goods must be capable of **passing without objection** in the trade under the contract description. [U.C.C. §2-314(2)(a)]

~할 수 있는 / 이의

- "Fungible goods" are those that can be **interchanged without comment** (like grain commingled in a grain elevator); the owner does not care whether the original goods are returned as long as a like quantity is delivered. In the case of fungible goods, to be "merchantable," the goods must be of "fair average quality"; i.e., the bulk

대체가능한 상품, 대체물
곡물 / 혼합하다
대량

(not the whole) of the goods must hover around the middle belt of quality. [U.C.C. §2-314(2)(b)] — 공중을 맴돌다, 상회하다 / 중간정도의 품질, 중등품질*

- To be merchantable, goods must also be "**fit for the ordinary purposes** for which such goods are used." [U.C.C. §2-314(2)(c)] This is by far the most important standard of "merchantability".
- It is also required that the goods "run within the variations permitted by the agreement, of even kind, quality, and quantity within each unit and among all units involved." [U.C.C. §2-314(2)(d)]. — 동일(균일)한 종류
- Goods must also be "**adequately contained, packaged, and labeled** as the agreement may require." [U.C.C. §2-314(2)(e)] — 포함하다 / 표시하다
- Finally, to be merchantable goods must conform to the promises or affirmations of fact made on the container or label. [U.C.C. §2-314(2)(f)]

Caceci v. Di Canio Construction Corporate – N.Y. Ct. App., 72 N.Y.2d 521, 526 N.E.2d (1988)

The plaintiffs contracted with the defendant for a parcel of land on which a one-family ranch home was to be constructed. The defendant guaranteed the plumbing, heating, and electrical work, roof and basement walls for one year from title closing. When the kitchen floor started dripping four years later, the defendant unsuccessfully attempted to repair the cracks and dips in the floor. The plaintiffs sued for breached duties under negligence and implied warranty theories, and the trial court awarded damages for the reasonable cost of correcting defendant's slipshod performance. The Appellate Division affirmed solely on the implied warranty theory, holding that there was an implied term in the express contract between the builder-vendor and purchasers that the house be constructed in a skillful manner free from material defects. The defendant appealed.

parcel of land: 토지 한 필지 / plumbing: 배관 / attempted: 시도하다 / negligence: 과실, 부주의 / Appellate Division: 항소법원

Issue

* 우리 민법 제375조의 용어

Does the "Housing Merchant" warranty impose by legal implication a contractual liability on a homebuilder for skillful performance and quality of a newly constructed home?

Holding and Reasoning

Yes. The doctrine that the buyer must beware may not be invoked by the defendant, a builder-seller, against the plaintiffs, the purchasers. Homes contracted for sale prior to construction involve an agreement between the parties who generally do not bargain as equals. Inspection of the premises is impossible, especially with respect to latent defects. Thus, the purchaser has no meaningful choice but to rely on the builder-vendor to deliver what was bargained for – a house reasonably fit for the purpose for which it was intended. The affirmed award of damages after a nonjury trial must be upheld.

주의, 주목하다

조사 / 토지, 부동산, 건물이 딸린 토지

신뢰하다, 의지하다

II. Implied Warranty of Fitness

If a seller has reason to know of the particular use of goods contemplated by the buyer, and is also aware that the buyer is relying on the seller's judgment to select suitable goods, then an implied warranty of fitness for that particular use or purpose arises, unless specifically excluded by the seller. [U.C.C. §2-315]

숙고하다

계약의 목적에 관한 보증

D. Disclaimer of Warranties

I. Disclaiming Express Warranties

"Words or conduct relevant to the creation of an express warranty and words or conduct tending to negate or limit warranty shall be **construed wherever reasonable as consistent with each other**; but subject to the provisions of this Article on parol or extrinsic evidence (section 2-202), negation or limitation is inoperative to the extent that such construction is unreasonable." [U.C.C. §2-316]

~하는 경향이 있다 / 부정하다

해석하다

구두의 / 외부의

II. Disclaiming Implied Warranties

Because implied warranties arise apart from any agreement of the parties, the parties are given greater latitude to limit or disclaim liability arising therefrom. Subsections (2) and (3) of U.C.C. §2-316 list some ways that implied (but not express) warranties can be disclaimed. 발생하다 허용범위, 폭

1. By Specific Language

The seller may rely on clauses in the sales contract that disclaim liability for implied warranties. However, the U.C.C. imposes certain requirements for disclaiming the two basic implied warranties, merchantability and fitness for particular purpose.

2. Disclaiming the Implied Warranty

An **oral disclaimer** (sufficient to disclaim merchantability), is **not sufficient** to exclude the implied warranty of fitness for particular purpose. The particular purpose disclaimer must be in writing, and the writing must be "conspicuous". 현저한, 눈에 띄는

3. Timing the Disclaimer

The disclaiming language must be part of the offer and acceptance process to be effective. A disclaimer delivered after the contract is in existence comes too late to have any effect, unless the buyer agrees to the modification. 변경

E. Remedies For Breach of Warranty

I. Before Acceptance

If a breach of warranty occurs prior to acceptance of the goods, the breach is treated like any other failure to perform the contract. The buyer may reject the goods for this reason, demand specific performance, cover, or measure damages according to various U.C.C. formulas. 발생하다

II. After Acceptance

Once the buyer has accepted the goods, the U.C.C.

provides that the buyer may recover any loss in value of the goods because of the breach [U.C.C. §2-714(l)] plus consequential and incidental damages where proper [U.C.C. §2-714(3)]. In appropriate circumstances, the buyer may revoke acceptance and recover damages.

규정하다

취소하다, 철회하다

1. Loss in Value of Goods

The standard measure of value in goods in a breach of warranty suit is the difference, at the time and place of acceptance, between the value of the goods accepted and the value they would have had if they had been as warranted. [U.C.C. §2-714(l)]

경우, 소송

2. Consequential Damages

Often the loss of value of goods will represent only a part of the buyer's loss. Thus the U.C.C. follows the rule of Hadley v. Baxendale (see infra), and imposes liability where the seller at the time of contract had reason to know of additional loss that would result from a failure to meet the buyer's needs or requirements. [U.C.C. §2-715(2)(a)]

Hadley v. Baxendale, 156 Eng. Rep. 145 (1854)

Hadley owns a mill. The crank shaft broke and he urgently needed a new one because the mill was stopped otherwise. Hadley hired Baxendale to take the broken shaft to the engineer so that a new one could be made. Baxendale promised next-day delivery. However, he delayed in sending the shaft, and so the mill was shut down for several days. Hadley sued for lost profits. Baxendale claimed the damages were too remote. The trial court found for Hadley.

크랭크 축

납품, 배달 / 지체하다

제소하다 / 일실이익

관련성이 희박한 / 사실심 (1심) 법원

Issue

Is a breaching party liable for the other's lost profits?

Holding and Reasoning

The damages to be awarded are the damages resulting from the breach which the parties could reasonably contemplate at the time of contract formation.

고려하다, 숙고하다

The court reasoned that Hadley would be entitled to lost profits if he had clearly communicated that to Baxendale. Then the parties could have negotiated a contract based on this special circumstance. Baxendale had no reason to believe that the mill would be down during the time that the crank shaft was in his hands. This was not the normal course of business. Thus, Baxendale should not be liable for lost profits.

협상하다, 흥정하다

3. Incidental Damages

Finally, the buyer may also recover any cost or **expense reasonably incurred incidental** to the seller's delay or delivery of defective goods, e.g., storage or inspection charges, return freight, costs of cover, etc. [U.C.C. §2-715(l)]

저장 / 조사비용
반송운임

Diagram 4

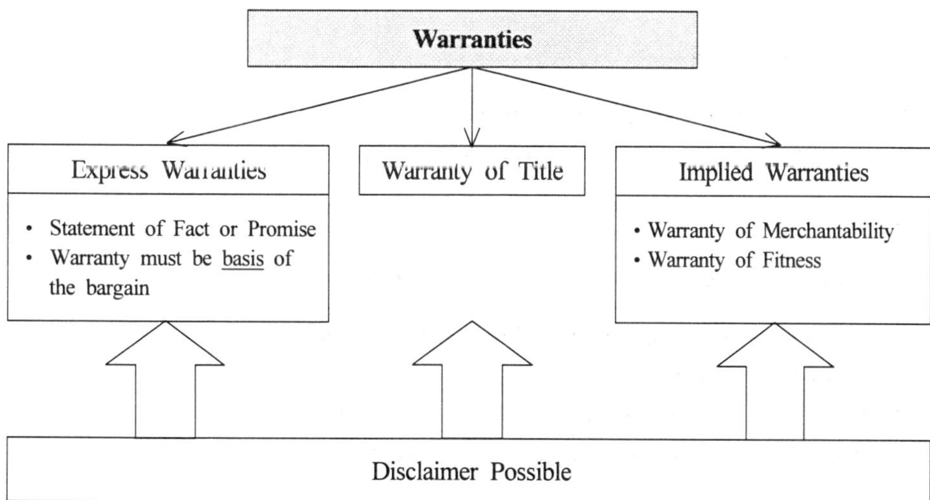

Further reading

McGovern/Lawrence, Contracts and Sales: Cases and Problems (1986); Lawrence, Understanding Sales and Leases of Goods (1996); King e.a., Sales Law; Alces/Hansford, Sales, Leases and Bulk Transfers (1989).

Chapter Five

Law of Torts

Part 1: Law of Torts

A. Intentional Torts

I. Intent

If the plaintiff wants to establish a **prima facie** case for intentional tort liability, it is necessary that he proves three elements: 언뜻 보기에, 첫눈에, 一見

- **act by the defendant**
- **intent** 고의, 의도
- **causation**

1. Act by the Defendant

Which act by the defendant is required depends on the kind of tort, e.g. battery, assault etc. Details are discussed below. 폭행, 상해 / 폭행위협, 상해위협, 단순폭행

2. Specific and General Intent

The defendant's intent may either be **specific** or **general**:

- **Specific intent** means that the defendant's goal in acting is to bring about certain consequences.
- **General intent** is present if the defendant is substantially certain that the consequences he intended will result.

Van Camp v. McAfoos – 156 NW2d 878 (1968)

Van Camp, a pedestrian on a sidewalk, was struck on the leg by a tricycle driven by McAfoos. Van Camp brought suit against McAfoos for the injury inflicted, however neither negligence nor willful or wrongful conduct on the part of McAfoos was alleged. 보행자 / 보도 삼륜자전거 (상해 등을) 가하다

* Battery의 경우 실제로 신체적인 가해행위가 있어야 하는 반면, assault(폭행의 협박)의 경우는 타인에게 두려움을 주는 것만으로도 범죄가 성립한다. assault는 경우에 따라 단순폭행(simple assault)의 의미로도 쓰인다.

Van Camp <u>asserted</u> that invasion of her person was sufficient by itself for her <u>cause of action</u>. The trial court <u>sustained</u> McAfoos' <u>motion for dismissal</u>, due to the absence of any allegation of fault on his part.

주장하다
제소원인, 제소이유
지지하다, 승인하다 / 각하 또는 기각신청

<u>Issue</u>

Must a plaintiff generally allege <u>fault</u> on the defendant's part to establish a cause of action for personal injuries?

유책함, 책임있음

<u>Holding and Reasoning</u>

Yes. All essential elements of a cause of action must be pleaded to establish a prima facie case. Here, the plaintiff did not plead any facts indicating wrongful action or fault on the part of the defendant. In situations such as this, there is no liability without proof of fault.

An action for <u>personal injuries</u> must generally include ultimate facts giving rise to an allegation of some fault on the defendant's part.

인사 상해

The plaintiff here attempted to place the defendant's conduct into the category of a <u>strict liability tort</u>, where no proof of fault is required.

엄격한 위험책임

3. Transferred Intent

According to the doctrine of **<u>transferred intent</u>** the defendant, who acts in such a way that the intended injury would be actionable, is liable for all direct consequences even though they are not intended.

전가된 고의

Example: Defendant fires a pistol intending to put A in apprehension of an immediate and unconsented-to bodily touching but intending no actual touching. Without defendant's fault, the bullet actually strikes A. Defendant is liable to A for battery although he never intended a battery at all.

The theory of transferred intent requires that the tort intended and the tort that happens are both within the following list:

- <u>Assault</u> 폭행(의 협박)

- ▸ Battery 신체상해
- ▸ False imprisonment 감금죄
- ▸ Trespass to land 점유침해(부동산)
- ▸ Trespass to chattels 점유침해(동산)

Alteiri v. Colasso – Sup. Ct. of Conn., 362 A2d 798 (1975)

Alteiri was struck in the eye by an object thrown by Colasso. Colasso had thrown the object with the intent to scare a third person. Colasso alleged that Alteiri's suit was actually one for negligence, and that as such it was barred by a one-year statute of limitations. The complaint was filed within the three-year statute of limitations applicable to battery.

scare: 무섭게 하다
statute of limitations / complaint: 시효 / 고소, 고발

Issue

Where one is injured as a result of an attempted assault upon another by an actor, is the actor liable for battery to the person injured?

Holding and Reasoning

Yes. Under the doctrine of transferred intent, when one attempts to injure another but injures a third person instead, he is liable in battery to the person actually injured. This doctrine applies as well to assault actions. When one acts to place another in apprehension of bodily harm and injures a third person as a result, he is liable to the third person for battery. Here, even though Colasso intended to scare a third person, he is liable to Altieri for battery for the injury inflicted as a result of his attempted assault.

apprehension / bodily harm: 우려, 염려 / 신체적 상해
inflicted / attempted assault: (상해 등을) 가하다 / 폭행협박의 미수

When one intends to assault another but causes injury to a third person instead, the intent for the assault will be deemed transferred so as to render the actor liable to the injured person for battery.

deemed: 간주하다

II. Battery

If the plaintiff wants to establish a prima facie case for battery, **harmful or offensive contact must be proven**.

harmful / offensive: 아픔을 주는 / 공격적인

Liability for battery is invoked if

- the defendant acts intending to cause a harmful or offensive contact with the person of the other or a third person, and
- a harmful contact of the other directly or indirectly results.

1. Offensive contact

But what is the meaning of offensive contact? If one shakes another one's hand too strongly and he is hurt, does that automatically leads to a battery case? – Obviously not. However, sometimes it is difficult to distinguish between **socially accepted touching** and **actionable batteries**. Therefore, courts require that the defendant intends to cause harmful or offensive contact.

a) Definition

Offensive contact is unpermitted contact as thought by an average person. The social norms play the decisive role. The contact is seen within a frame of reference. Therefore, it is not necessary that contact is harmful. It is also tortuous if it is offensive or nonconsensual.

평균인
준기(準據)
불법행위의

b) Criteria

A bodily contact is offensive if it offends a reasonable sense of personal dignity. In order that a contact be offensive to a reasonable sense of personal dignity, it must be one which **would offend the ordinary person and as such one not unduly sensitive as to his personal dignity**. It must be a contact which is unwarranted by the social usages prevalent at the time and place at which it is inflicted.

개인의 존엄
일반적으로 통용되는

A more subjective standard leaves open the risk that some people will consider every little touch offensive. The defendant, under this test, is not liable to a hyper-sensitive person unless he is aware of the plaintiff's condition.

과도하게 민감한

c) Extended Personality

The plaintiff is also touched if the defendant touches some intimate extension of the plaintiff's person, as when the defendant jerks a plate from plaintiff's hand, even if the hand itself is not touched. 갑자기 잡아당기다

Fisher v. Carrousel Motor Hotel — 424 S.W.2d 627 (Tex.1967)

The plaintiff, a black man, was approached by an agent of Carrousel Motor Hotel while attending a lunch at the hotel. The hotel employee "forcibly dispossessed" the plaintiff of a plate he was holding and shouted in a loud and offensive manner, saying that Negroes were not served in the hotel. 빼앗다, 강탈하다

Issue

Is there a cause of action for battery?

Holding and Reasoning

Yes. The Appeals Court held that there was no assault, since the plaintiff admitted that he never suffered fear or apprehension of physical injury, but the claim of battery was upheld. The court said "personal indignity is the essence of an action for battery; and consequently the defendant is liable not only for contacts which do actual physical harm, but also for those which are offensive and insulting."

항소법원
당하다, 고통받다
우려, 염려
존엄성을 해침, 모독, 모욕

Note: It is important to remember that the requisite elements of battery must still be present. That is to say, offensive and insulting conduct cannot constitute a battery in the absence of intent and contact. 모욕하다

2. Intent

We have already talked about the requirement of "intent". In Vosberg the court decided that the intent needed is just the intent to contact.

Vosberg v. Putney — 50 NW 403 (Wis. 1891)

Plaintiff had previously injured his leg above the knee

about 1 1/2 months before defendant reached across the classroom aisle with his foot, and kicked plaintiff in the shin just below the knee. The kick was slight, however the jury found that plaintiff developed tissue and bone damage as a result of the kick, by aggravating the infection originating during the previous injury. The jury also found that defendant did not mean to do plaintiff any harm.

정강이
가벼운
조직
악화시키다

The plaintiff brought an action to recover damages for assault and battery. The first trial resulted in judgment for plaintiff for $2,800. Defendant appealed to this court, where the previous judgment was reversed for error, and a new trial awarded.

(손해배상을) 받다
판결
항소하다
파기환송하다
인정하다, 주다(여기서는 판결을 얻다)

Issue

Is the intent to contact another enough for a cause of action in battery?

Holding and Reasoning

Yes. Since the kick was a violation of the "order and decorum" of the school classroom, it was unlawful, and therefore the intention to commit it was unlawful. Because the classroom had rules of "order and decorum", and the teacher had already called the class to order, there was no "implied license" because kicking another in the shin is not expected behavior for the classroom.

침해
범하다

A wrong-doer is liable for all injuries resulting directly from the wrongful act, whether they could or could not have been foreseen by him.

Another specification can be found in the 1955 case of **Garrat v. Dailey**.

Garratt v. Dailey – Sup. Ct. of Wash., 279 P2d 1091 (1955)

Defendant Dailey, a 5 year old child, moved a chair in which the plaintiff Garratt was about to sit. Garratt started to sit, and fell to the ground fracturing her hip and incurring other injuries. Garratt alleged that Dailey deliberately pulled

부수다 / (손실, 상해를) 입다
주장하다 / 고의로

the chair from under her, knowing she was about to sit. Dailey argued that he moved the chair for his own use, and that he tried to replace it when he saw that Garratt was about to sit where the chair had been. 대체하다

The trial court accepted Dailey's version, and rendered judgment in his favor without findings as to his knowledge at the time of his act. 1심법원

Issue

Is the intentional doing of an act which causes harmful or offensive contact with another sufficient by itself to constitute battery? 고의의

Holding and Reasoning

No. For a battery cause of action to be established, there must be proof that the defendant either acted for the purpose of causing contact with the plaintiff, or, that he knew that such contact was substantially certain to be produced. 목적

Here, there was no trial court consideration concerning whether Dailey knew with substantial certainty when he moved the chair that Garratt intended to sit where the chair had been. 고려

Since this must be established for a proper adjudication, the case is remanded back to the trial court for such a determination. 적절한 판결, 평가 / (사건을) 하급법원에 환송, 반송하다 / 확정

There are fine lines drawn between acts which are intentional, versus reckless, versus negligent. Battery requires intentional conduct, which the actor desires to produce harmful or offensive contact, or which he realizes has a substantial certainty of producing such contact. Also, note here that the age of the defendant would not automatically absolve him of liability, but would be significant in determining what he knew at the time of the conduct at issue 고의의 / 배려없는, 무모한 / 과실의, 부주의한 / 사면하다, 면책하다

3. Causation

To be liable for battery the defendant must have caused the injury. The "**But for**"-Test is applicable to find out if there is causation. 인과관계

a) Extent

The defendant is liable for all harm resulting from his contact with the person. Someone who deliberately violates the bodily integrity of another takes the risk that his acts will produce a harm greater than or different from the one intended.

온전함, 건강한 상태
손해, 상해, 고통

b) Thin skull rule

The defendant takes the plaintiff as he finds him. The defendant is liable for any consequences which ensue if there was sufficient intent for a claim of battery.

뒤이어 발생하다

Diagram 5

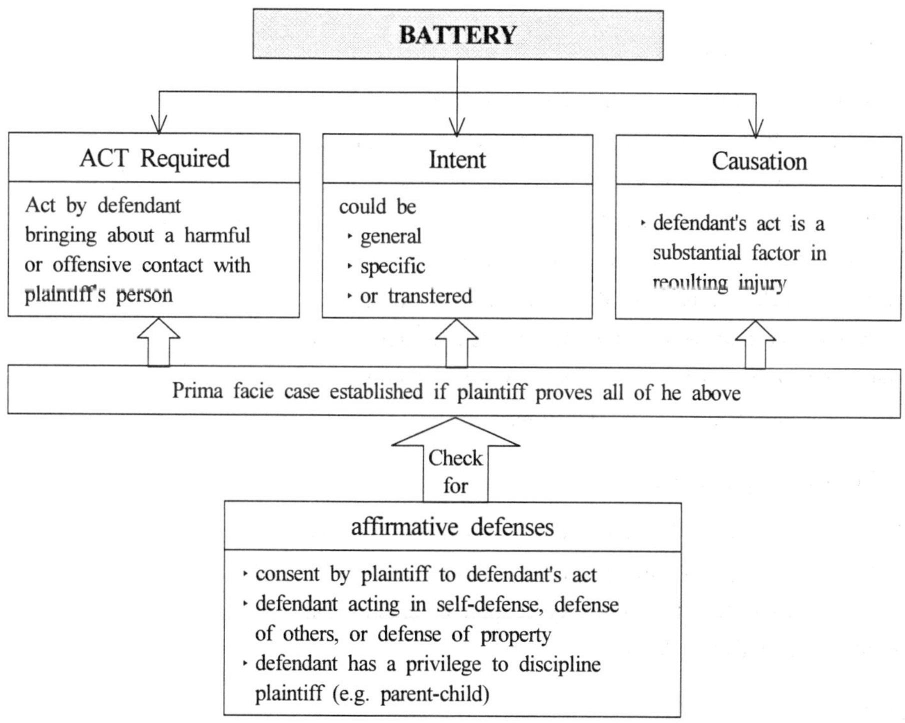

III. Assault

Assault is an act that is intended to and does place the plaintiff in apprehension of an immediate touching that would amount to a battery. The plaintiff's subjective recognition or apprehension that he is about to be touched in an impermis-

우려, 염려
주관적 인식

sible way is at the core of the assault claim.

Thus, the plaintiff has to prove the following elements:

- An act by the defendant creating a reasonable apprehension in plaintiff of immediate harmful or offensive conduct to plaintiff's person 즉시의
- Intent
- Causation

1. Apprehension

In determining whether the apprehension in a given case is reasonable, the courts usually apply a **reasonable person test.** Therefore, the court asks if a reasonable and prudent person would have reacted or felt like the plaintiff did. (사실 관계를) 확정하다 / 합리적인 사람

a) No hostility required

A joke that results in reasonable apprehension by the plaintiff is sufficient for assault. Furthermore, if one is attempting to batter but misses, he is liable for assault if the plaintiff is placed in apprehension of the blow. 시도하다 / 폭행하다 / 때림, 가격

Because assault only protects against fear of a harmful or offensive contact, **plaintiff must prove that he feared the type of contact that would support a battery claim if it actually occurred.** Thus, the meaning of "harmful or offensive" is also needed in assault cases. 두려움

b) Tests for apprehension

Assault protects not only against the fear of an unwelcome contact, but also against the anticipation or expectation of one. Apprehension here means the perception or anticipation of a blow, rather than a fright. 인지함 / 지각함

c) Awareness

For there to be an apprehension, the plaintiff must have been aware of the defendant's act. In battery the **plaintiff need not be aware** of the contact at the time thereof.

McCraney v. Flanagan – Ct. of App. of NC, 267 S.E.2d 404 (1980)

McCraney and Flanagan agreed to go for a ride in Flanagan's car to an unspecified location. They stopped on a dirt road and began to drink alcoholic beverages. Subsequently, they had intercourse. McCraney could not recall anything after her last drink, until she found herself away from the dirt road location. A medical examination revealed the presence of sperm in McCraney's vagina, and she subsequently brought suit against Flanagan for sexually assaulting her. The trial court granted Flanagan's motion for summary judgment, from which McCraney appealed.

성관계

성적 협박, 성폭력

Issue

Must a plaintiff be aware of a defendant's act for a tort action of assault to lie?

Holding and Reasoning

Yes. Here, the plaintiff admits that she does not recall any of the acts of the defendant upon which her complaint is based. The tort of assault occurs when one person puts another in apprehension of harmful or offensive contact. Apprehension of the plaintiff is the gravamen of the tort, and therefore, the plaintiff must be aware of the defendant's act at the time it takes place. Since McCraney was not aware of or in anticipation of Flanagan's act, she could not have experienced the requisite apprehension. Therefore, no assault action can lie, and the granting of summary judgment by the trial court was proper.

인정하다

(불법행위의) 핵심되는 사항

경험하다

In order for an action for assault to exist, the plaintiff must have been placed in apprehension of harmful or offensive contact by the defendant, and thus the plaintiff must have been aware of the defendant's allegedly tortuous act at the time it took place.

d) Imminent

Apprehended contact must be imminent – that is the defendant's act must cause the victim to apprehend that he is about to be touched. Thus, imminent means there is **no significant delay.** If it is not imminent the person can get a way.

즉각의, 즉시의

곧 신체접촉이 있을 것이다

지체

Dickens v. Puryear – 276 S.E.2d 325 (N.C. 1981)

The plaintiff Dickens had for some time shared alcohol, drugs, and sex with the seventeen-year-old daughter of the defendant Puryear. On one occasion, Puryear and four accomplices lured Dickens to a rural area, where Puryear pointed a gun at Dickens and cut his hair. The accomplices beat Dickens severely, and threatened with Puryear to either castrate or kill him. Puryear eventually allowed Dickens to go free, but threatened to kill him if he did not leave the state. Dickens brought suit against Puryear for intentional infliction of emotional distress during the third year after the incident, and thus within the three year statute of limitations for such actions. Puryear made a motion for summary judgment, on the basis that the complaint was actually for assault and battery, and that as such it was barred by the one year statute of limitations applicable to those torts. The trial court granted Puryear's motion.

연루자, 한 패 / 꾀어내다
거세하다
고의적인 감정장애 유발 행위
시효
약식재판

Issue

Are threats of future bodily harm actionable as assaults?

Holding and Reasoning

No. In order for a defendant to be liable for assault, he must place another in apprehension of imminent harmful or offensive contact. Threats of future harm are simply not within the purview of assault, and are actionable if at all--as intentional inflictions of mental distress, not as assault. Since Puryear threatened Dickens with future harm, obviously such cannot reasonably be characterized as creating apprehension of imminent harm, but rather as a threat intended to inflict serious mental distress.

영역

Inasmuch as the complaint properly stated a cause of action for intentional infliction of mental distress, the trial court should not have granted the defendant's summary judgment motion. A defendant is only liable for assault if he places a victim in apprehension of imminent harmful or offensive contact; threats of future harm are not enough.

소
약식재판에서의 청구

e) Words

Because of the requirement of "imminent", many courts have said that **words alone can not constitute an assault.** Words alone do not make the actor liable for assault unless together with other acts or circumstances they put the other in reasonable apprehension of an imminent harmful or offensive contact with his person. Thus, words alone are not sufficient. There must be some other conduct to allege an assault (shaking fists, etc.) 주먹을 흔들다

2. Intent

Defendant must act with the purpose to cause apprehension of a contact or substantial certainty that an action will result. Defendant may not avoid liability by claiming he did not mean to place the plaintiff in fear of unwanted touching, if it was foreseeable that defendant's act would result in reasonable apprehension in the plaintiff. 피하다 예측가능한

Diagram 6

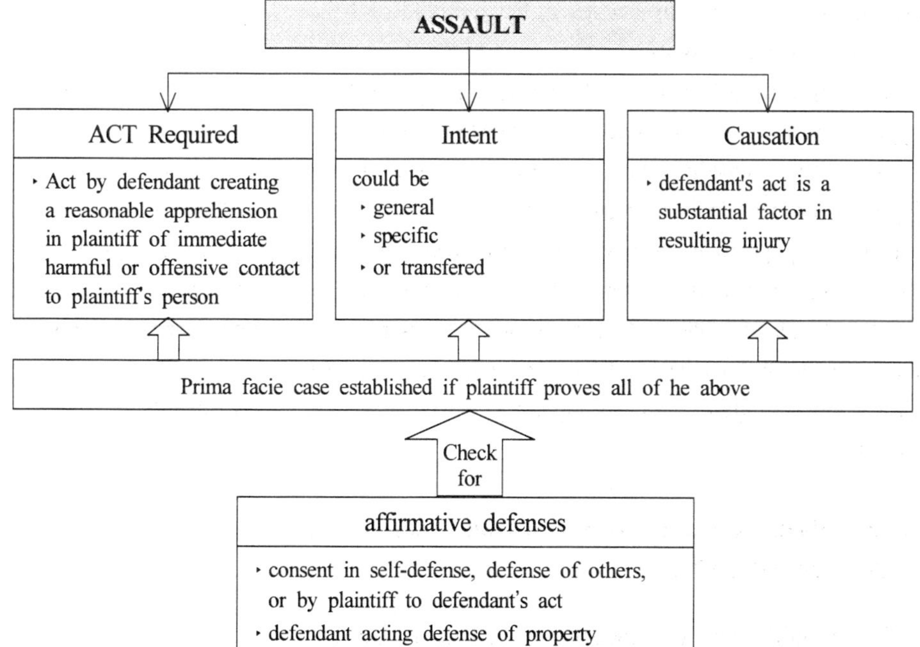

IV. False Imprisonment

Courts protect **personal freedom of movement** by imposing liability for false imprisonment. To establish a prima facie case the plaintiff must prove that the defendant intentionally confined or instigated the confinement of the plaintiff. The following four elements must be proven:

신체이동의 자유

충동, 교사하다 / 구속, 구금

- act by the defendant
- intent to obstruct or detain
- confinement
- causation

막다, 차단하다 / 못가게 붙들다

1. Methods of Confinement

One can distinguish between various methods of confinement. If a person is obstructed, but allowed to move his person in another direction of his own freewill he is not falsely imprisoned.

The means of escape must be unreasonable. There is no false imprisonment if an athletic person were locked in a room on the first floor with a window, but it would be if he were left without his clothes.

탈출방법, 가능성

False imprisonment will result where the plaintiff is restrained by the use of physical force directed at him or a member of his immediate family. False imprisonment can arise from direct or indirect threats of force.

제한하다

~로부터 발생하다

Short of any physical restraints, an officer may effectuate a confinement merely by asserting authority to do so. If the plaintiff submits to a law enforcement officer's assertion of authority to detain him, he has been confined, and unless the officer enjoys a privilege or an immunity he is liable for false arrest.

(경찰) 관리 / 실시하다, 행하다

(~에) 복종하다 / 주장

특권 / 면책특권

Great Atlantic & Pacific Tea Co. v. Paul – Sup. Ct. of Md, 261 A2d 731 (1970)

While plaintiff, Paul, was shopping at defendant's store, a store employee detained him under the suspicion that he had

못가게 붙들다 / 의심

shoplifted a can of tick spray. A search of Paul's person revealed no can of tick spray. Paul brought suit against defendant for falsely accusing him of shoplifting and unlawfully detaining him. Defendant argued that a shopkeeper should be privileged to detain and investigate with respect to an individual suspected of shoplifting.

(가게) 좀도둑질하다 / 진드기 스프레이
부당하게 혐의를 가지다

Issue

Is a shopkeeper without probable cause privileged to detain an individual who is suspected by the shopkeeper of shoplifting?

Holding and Reasoning

No. The necessary elements for a case of false imprisonment are a deprivation of the liberty of another without his consent and without legal justification.

박탈

Although the defendant urges the court to adopt the Restatement (Second) of Torts privilege in favor of persons who detain and investigate as to individuals suspected of theft, no such privilege is found in Maryland law.

특권
구속하다 / 조사하다

In Maryland, a shopkeeper has only the rights of a private person, and a private person can only arrest for felonies, and misdemeanors amounting to a breach of peace. Since shoplifting is generally a misdemeanor which is not disorderly or dangerous to the public peace, neither the private person nor the shopkeeper has the power to arrest suspected shoplifters.

중범죄, 무거운 범죄
경범자 / 공공질서위반

Although there is a common law exception for a property owner who detains one suspected of taking his property, the property owner does so at his peril, and is liable for false imprisonment if the detainee does not in fact have the property. Here, the facts proved that the detention went beyond what was necessary to ascertain the true facts.

예외
위험
수감인
(사실을) 확인하다

In fact, the store employee involved never saw Paul take anything, and Paul had not shown any intention of leaving the store without paying for anything. In a self-service store, no probable cause exists to detain unless a suspect attempts to leave the store without paying, or unless he has exercised unequivocal control over the property.

시도
명백한

2. Insufficient Forms of Confinement

It is not enough if the defendant puts moral pressure on the plaintiff with the result that he remains in the area. The same is true for future threats.

윤리적 압력

3. No Need to Resist

The plaintiff is **not under the obligation to resist** the force that is applied to confine him.

저항할 의무를 지지 않는

Hardy v. Labelle's Distributing Co. – Sup. Ct. of Mont., 661 P2d 53 (1983)

The plaintiff Hardy, a new employee at Labelle's Distributing Co. (defendant), was accused by another employee of stealing a watch. Hardy was subsequently escorted to the store manager's office by the assistant manager, after being told that she was being taken on a tour of the store. Police and store officials in the room accused Hardy of stealing a watch, a charge which she denied. Hardy agreed to take a lie detector test, and passed it. She subsequently brought this suit against the defendants, for false imprisonment during the time she was questioned about the watch. Hardy appealed from a trial court judgment against her.

근로자
(~한 혐의로) 고소를 받다
(죄의) 비난
항소를 제기하다
이동의 자유

Issue

Does false imprisonment exist when an individual's freedom of movement is not restrained against her will?

Holding and Reasoning

No. The two key elements of false imprisonment are the restraint of an individual against her will, and the unlawfulness of such restraint. Here, there was no showing that Hardy was restrained against her will. Although she alleged that she felt compelled to remain in the store manager's office, she also admitted that she wanted to stay there and clear herself. She never asked to leave, nor was

주장하다 / 강제하다

she ever told that she couldn't. Since Hardy was never threatened or forced to stay in the office, no false imprisonment action can lie.

There is no false imprisonment when an individual's freedom of movement is not restrained against her will.

Diagram 7

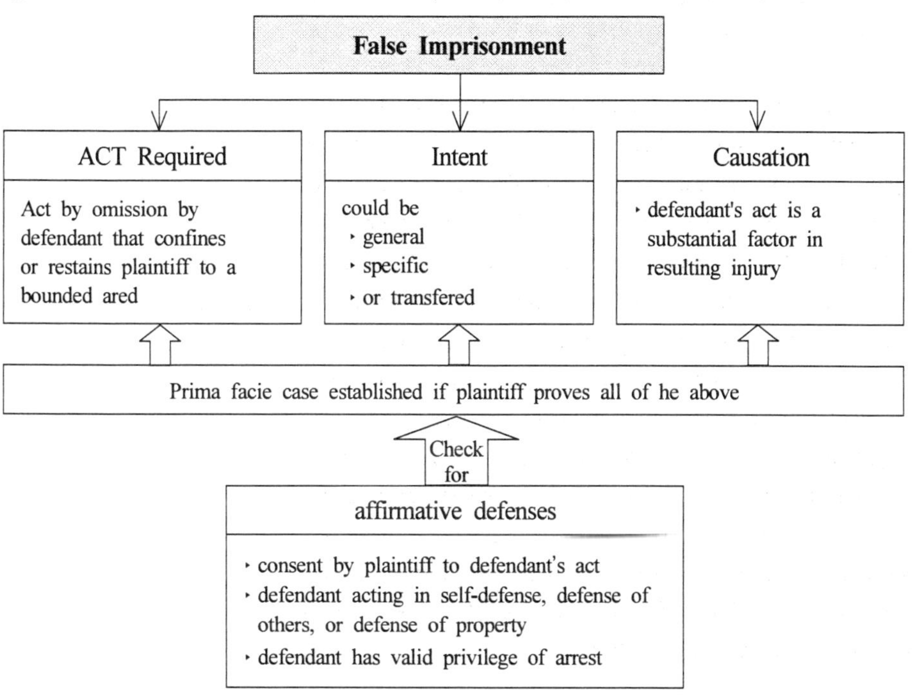

V. Intentional Infliction of Emotional Distress

The Restatement of Law defines this tort as follows: One who by **extreme and outrageous** conduct intentionally or recklessly causes severe emotional distress to another is subject to liability for such emotional distress, and if bodily harm to the other results from it, for such bodily harm.

난폭한, 무법의
무모하게, 배려없이 / 격렬한 / 장애, 위험

Thus, the plaintiff must prove the following four elements to establish a prima facie case for intentional infliction of emotional distress:

- ▶ Defendant's extreme and outrageous conduct
- ▶ intent or recklessness
- ▶ causation

▸ damage = severe emotional distress

1. Extreme and Outrageous Conduct

The extreme conduct must be severe and it exceeds all bounds which could be tolerated by society. 초과하다, 넘어서다

LaBrier v. Anheuser Ford, Inc. – Miss. Ct. of App., 612 SW2d 790 (1981)

James LaBrier was an employee at defendant Anheuser Ford, Inc. He was scheduled to be away from his employment for several weeks, and decided to take his demonstrator automobile with him -- without the permission of Anheuser Ford. Shortly thereafter, officials of Anheuser Ford visited the LaBrier residence to retrieve the automobile, finding only plaintiff Mrs. LaBrier at home. They questioned her extensively as to her husband's whereabouts, threatening legal action against him in loud and angry tones of voice perceptible to witnesses. Mrs. LaBrier – who was under medical care for emotional problems – became upset, began to cry, and experienced swollen and itching eyes as well as a body rash. She brought suit against Anheuser Ford as a result of the behavior of its officials, and appealed from a trial court directed verdict against her.

되찾다, 회복하다

지각할 수 있는, 들을 수 있는

1심 법원

Issue

Is a defendant liable for intentional infliction of mental distress if he verbally threatens and abuses another in front of others, knowing of the victim's fragile emotional state?

위협하다, 협박하다

Holding and Reasoning

Yes. Intentional infliction of mental distress requires an intentional act of extreme and outrageous conduct on the part of a defendant. Under the right circumstances, verbal abuse of an emotionally fragile person, in the presence of others, could be characterized as extreme and outrageous conduct. Here, the actions of the Anheuser Ford officials in using loud and threatening language to harass and humiliate the plaintiff might be deemed extreme and outrageous, particularly in light

남용

괴롭히다, 희롱하다 / 굴욕감을 주다

of their knowledge of her emotional illness. Furthermore, such knowledge could lead a jury to find that the actions of the defendants were intentional. In light of these facts, the plaintiff's case should have gone to the jury, and a directed verdict was improper.

A defendant may be liable for intentional infliction of mental distress if he verbally abuses another before witnesses, with knowledge of such person's peculiar emotional sensitivities.

2. Intent and Transferred Intent

The defendant will be liable not only for intentional conduct but also for **reckless conduct**, i.e. acting in reckless disregard of a high probability that emotional distress will result.

(타인을 도무지) 배려하지 않는

There is no transfer of intent with regard to intentional infliction of emotional distress. If the defendant attempts to commit a different intentional tort and the only result is the plaintiff's emotional distress, there is no intentional infliction of emotional distress.

Diagram 8

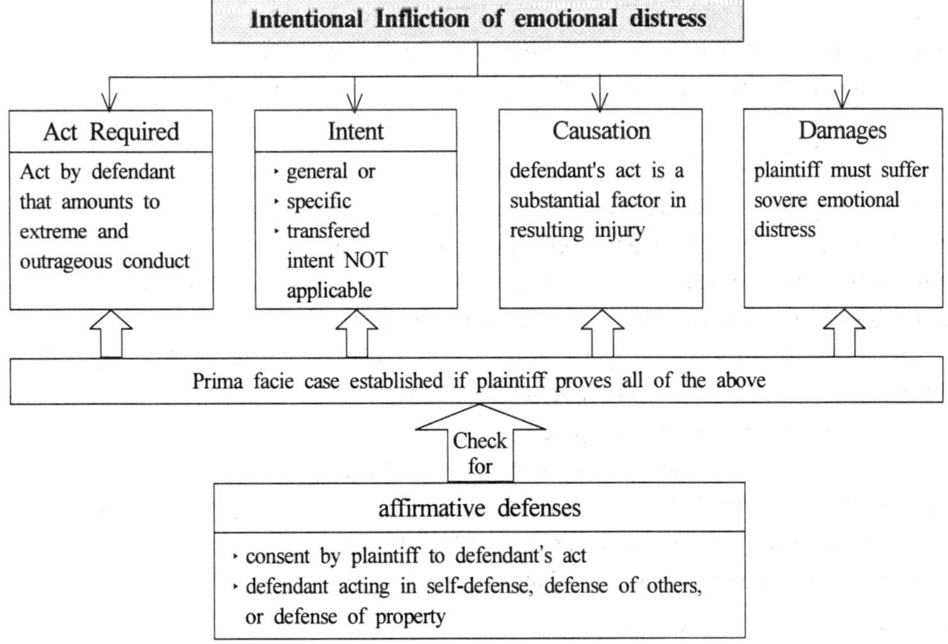

VI. Trespass

One who intentionally enters or causes **direct and tangible entry upon the land in possession of another** is a trespasser and liable for the tort of trespass, unless the entry is privileged or consented to. To establish a pima facie case* the plaintiff must prove the following:

만질 수 있는, 유형의

특권있는 / 동의를 받은 / "일단 유리한 사건", "일견 증명된 사건"을 성립시키다

- physical invasion of plaintiff's real property
- intent
- causation

1. Physical Invasion

There are mainly three interests protected by the tort of trespass to land:

부동산 점유침해(비교, 주거 침입)

- the right to exclusive possession of land
- the right of physical integrity of the land itself
- the right to the use and enjoyment of the land

향유, (권리의) 보유

The defendant does not need to personally enter the plaintiff's land. He may throw a rock onto the land or push someone on it. Some object must go on the land as a result of the defendant's action. Even if defendant had permission to enter plaintiff's land it is trespass if he refuses to leave.

허가
거절하다

2. Entries above the Surface

Possessory interests are not limited to the surface of the land. They also include the right to exclusive possession of **reasonably usable airspace** above the ground as well as **space below the surface**. Thus, it was held that it was trespass to intrude upon non-navigable waters on the land, to fire a bullet across it, to maintain a utility line above it, or even to extend an arm into the airspace.

점유권

(지표위) 공중의 공간

운송할 수 있는 / 운송가능한

(에너지 등의) 공급라인

Thus, another modern use of trespass is to challenge pollution or other introduction of noxious substances onto one's land or the airspace over it. Courts have allowed claims of trespass in cases where smoke or pollution has entered the

유독성의, 독이 있는

* 반증이 없는 한 일단 진실한 것으로 추정되어 승소할 수 있는 사례를 prima facie(프리마 파치에) case라고 한다.

plaintiff's land and has caused damage.

3. Intent

The intent requirement for trespass is only that the trespasser intended to enter the property. It is irrelevant whether he knew that the property belonged to the plaintiff, or even if he believed it was his own property. 속하다, ~의 소유하다

Diagram 9

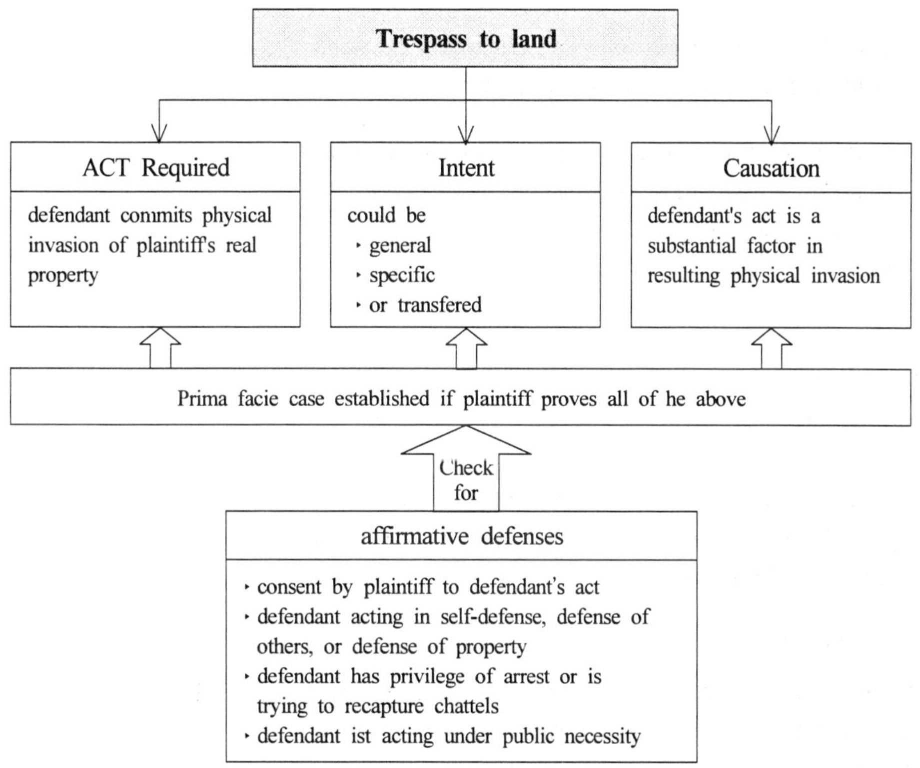

VII. Trespass to Chattel and Conversion

(동산의) 횡령

The tort of trespass to chattel is committed by intentionally interfering with the plaintiff's possession in a way that causes recognizable harm.

1. Trespass to Chattel

For a prima facie case the following four elements must be present: 일견 증명된 사례, 일단 유리한 상황

- ▸ Interference with plaintiff's right of possession 방해, 침해
- ▸ Intent
- ▸ Causation
- ▸ Damage

The defendant may interfere with the plaintiff's access or use or by causing actual harm to the chattel.

2. Conversion

A plaintiff must prove the following elements if he wants to establish a prima facie case for conversion: 입증하다

- ▸ **Interference with plaintiff's right of possession in the chattel** that is serious enough to warrant that the defendant pay the full value of the chattel
- ▸ Intent
- ▸ Causation

a) Dispossession

The defendant can commit conversion by any act that counts as dominion over the chattel and that is not privileged or protected by law. Dispossessing the plaintiff, or preventing the plaintiff's possession when he is entitled to it, is a common form of conversion. 지배

b) Destruction

Intentional destruction, major alteration, or serious damage is often an extreme case of dispossession and it counts as a conversion. 변경

If the defendant intermeddles with a chattel, without intent to cause harm to it but substantial harm or destruction nevertheless occurs, the defendant becomes a **converter liable for the destruction.** 소유권 침해자

c) Misdelivery

A warehouse or other bailee who holds the plaintiff's goods must deliver them only to the plaintiff or to persons the plaintiff designates. If the bailee misdelivers the goods to 창고 / 수탁업자, 수탁자 (反, bailor) 지정하다 / 잘못 배달하다,

the wrong person, even by honest mistake, he is a converter and liable for the value of the goods. 인도하다

d) The Bona Fide Purchaser of Converted Goods

If there is a bona fide purchaser of converted goods three scenarios have to be distinguished: 선의의 구매자 / 장물

- The innocent purchaser buys from a thief-converter. The purchaser is fully liable for conversion.
- The innocent purchaser buys from someone who obtained voidable title to the goods by fraud or other misdoings. The purchaser is not liable for conversion; his title is good and he retains the chattel without liability. 취소가능한 권리 / 기망, 사기 비행, 악행 되찾다, 회복하다
- The third scenario is governed by the U.C.C. Under U.C.C. §2-403 (2), it provides that if a person entrusts his goods to a "merchant who deals in goods of that kind", then the merchant has a power to transfer all the title the person had. Thus, the innocent purchaser is protected under the U.C.C.-rule. 맡기다, 위탁하다

3. Trespass to Chattels and Conversion

Conversion is one of the many common-law torts that relate to interference with possessory interests in personal property, called "chattels." It is closely associated with a "trespass to chattels" and is a more serious version of it. Thus, trespass to chattels is available for any intentional interference with personal property of any substantial kind, while conversion is an interference so serious that the value of the personal property is essentially lost to the original owner. ~와 연결되다

B. Defenses to Intentional Torts

For intentional tort cases one can mainly distinguish mainly four different defenses: consent, self-defense, defenses to property and recapture of chattels. 정당방위 동산의 회복

I. Consent

Consent can be used as a defense against any intentional tort when the plaintiff has **expressly** or impliedly agreed to the harm inflicted. Consent can also be **implied** when the plaintiff places himself in a situation where it is obvious that harm will result.

Either express or implied consent is effective to relieve the actor of responsibility for the acts addressed. (책임 등을) 경감하다, 면제하다

1. Capacity

One of the most important elements of consent is capacity. **Did the plaintiff have the capacity to consent?** The capacity to consent is important because the consenting person's rights are narrowed.

Minors, mentally incompetent or drunken persons are deemed incapable of consent to tortuous conduct. The plaintiff may not have consented if consent was obtained by duress, fraud, concealment, non-disclosure or exploitation by the defendant of a known plaintiff weakness. 미성년자 / 정신장애자 / 간주하다 / 강제 / 기망 / 침묵 / 착취

2. Express Consent

Express Consent to an act is a **subjective willingness for the act to occur.**

The consent may be a valid defense although the plaintiff expressly consents by mistake. It is invalid if the defendant caused the mistake.

Consent induced by fraud or duress generally is not a defense. The fraud or duress do not vitiate the consent if they are only about a “collateral” matter not going to the essential nature of the transaction. 손상하다, 해치다

3. Implied Consent

Implied Consent is conduct, including words, that are **reasonably understood by another as a reflection of consent.** 합리적으로 이해하다 / 반영, 생각을 내어 비침

A special form of consent by silence arises in the case of

social custom, as distinct from overt conduct of the plaintiff. 관습, 관행 / 명백한

4. Scope and Termination of Consent

Consent does not bar the plaintiff's claim for any tortuous conduct that is outside the scope of the consent or apparent consent nor for any tortuous conduct occurring after consent has been effectively revoked. 막다, 금지하다 / 범위, 틀 / 명백한, 분명한

The plaintiff may limit his consent as he likes, consenting to one act but not another, or to acts at one time, but not another, or to acts under some conditions but not others.

A plaintiff who gives consent may terminate or revoke it at any time by communicating the revocation to the person who may act upon the consent. A communicated revocation withdraws the defendant's privilege. 종료하다 / 철회, 취소하다

5. Consent to Medical Treatment

In surgery, the rule is that if the plaintiff consents to one particular surgery for one particular purpose it will not constitute consent to another different surgical procedure. 수술

Bailey v. Belinfante – Ct. of App. of Ga., 218 SE2d 289(1975)

At a hospital, Bailey signed a consent for Belinfante to perform tooth extraction, as well as "... procedures in addition to or different from those.., contemplated .... which... [Belinfante] may consider necessary.., in the course of the operation." Before the operation, Belinfante reviewed Bailey's records and determined that all (27) of his teeth should be extracted. Belinfante testified that he discussed this with Bailey and was given oral consent, whereas Bailey testified that he could not recollect such a discussion. Bailey had been given "pre-operative medicine" before surgery. Belinfante removed all (27) of Bailey's teeth, and Bailey brought this action for battery, asserting that no consent had been given for the removal of more than eleven teeth. The trial judge granted Belinfante's motion for directed verdict, and Bailey appealed.

(이빨을) 뽑아내다 / 숙고하다 / 서류, 기록 / 구두의 동의 / 기억하다 / 주장하다 / 항소하다

Issue

Is a surgeon liable for battery if he performs a procedure upon a patient which exceeds the scope of the consent obtained from the patient?

Holding and Reasoning

Yes. Generally, consent is a defense to an action for battery.

However this does not hold true when the consent parameters are overstepped. 한계를 넘다

Belinfante argues that he obtained consent twice in writing and once verbally from Bailey. With respect to the "consent" given at Belinfante's office, Bailey had the right to withdraw this up to the time of surgery. A jury could have found that the subsequent agreement for eleven teeth to be extracted rescinded the first "consent." The consent form signed at the hospital dealt with operations different from those contemplated which were deemed necessary "in the course of the operation." A jury could have found that this would only permit a different operation once surgery had begun. Finally, since the parties gave differing versions as to the alleged verbal consent prior to the surgery, a question of fact was created for the jury to resolve.

무효화하다, 철회하다

차이를 보이다 / 주장하다

II. Self Defense

The defendant is privileged to use **reasonable force to defend himself** against unprivileged acts that he reasonably believes will cause him bodily harm or offensive bodily contact.

합리적인
정당화되지 않은, (특별히) 허락된 것이 아닌

1. Retreat

In the usual case, the defendant may defend himself from harm by using **non-deadly force**, even if he could avoid injury by retreating or by complying with some improper demand asserted by the plaintiff even if his self-defense will inflict harm on the plaintiff.

사람을 죽일만한 정도의 물리력(non- 이에 대한 부정어)

But if the harm threatened is unintentional, merely the

result of the plaintiff's negligence, the defendant should reasonably avoid harm if possible, rather than inflict harm upon the negligent plaintiff. 과실, 부주의

2. Reasonable Force

The force used by the defendant in the exercise of his privilege must be reasonable under the circumstances as they reasonably appeared to the defendant. The force that is reasonable **depends in large measure upon the harm threatened and in some measure on the whole circumstances of the case.** 상황

III. Defense of Property

Generally, one may use reasonable force to prevent the commission of a tort against his property. The standard of reasonableness is a special one. 행함

1. Standard of Reasonableness

Brown v. Martinez – Sup. Ct. of New Mex., 361 P2d 152 (1961)

Brown and two other boys entered a farm occupied by Martinez for the purpose of stealing watermelons. Upon hearing Brown and his accomplices during their trespass, Martinez fired a rifle to scare them. A rifle bullet struck Brown in the leg however, causing serious injury. Brown and his father sued Martinez for these injuries, and the trial court dismissed their claim. 라이플 총 / 맞히다, 치다 / 기각하다

Issue

Is one permitted to use deadly force for the protection of property?

Holding and Reasoning

No. One is prohibited from resorting to the use of firearms to prevent a trespass or the commission of a non-felonious act. The law places a higher value upon human safety than upon mere rights in property. There is no privilege to use 금지하다, (~수단에) 도움을 청하다, 호소하다 / 중범죄의, 흉악한

force which is calculated to cause death or serious bodily injury where only property is threatened. However such force may be utilized when one's own "safety is threatened. Here, there was no suggestion that Martinez ever feared for his safety. Thus Martinez is liable for the injuries caused by his attempt to frighten Brown and his accomplices. 제안

One is not permitted to use deadly force to protect property, or to protect against a trespass, unless his personal safety is threatened.

2. Deadly Trap Rules

Unless criminal statutes provide otherwise, the defendant may **protect his dwelling place** by deadly traps against intruders who are in fact entering or attempting to enter in the course of a felony, provided deadly traps are otherwise reasonable. 거주지, 주거

Katko v. Briney – Sup. Ct. of Iowa, 183 N.W.2d 657 (1971)

Defendant Briney inherited a farm house which had been the target of a number of housebreakings. Briney and her husband boarded up the house, posted a no trespassing sign, and set up a shotgun trap in one of the rooms aimed at injuring the legs of anyone who entered. No warning of the gun was posted. Plaintiff Katko and an accomplice entered the house to find bottles and jars. As Katko entered the bedroom, the shotgun went off injuring him severely. Although acknowledging the illegality of his entry into the house, Katko brought suit against Briney for his injuries. Briney argued that the law permits the use of a spring gun trap for the purpose of prohibiting the unlawful entry into a dwelling.

상속하다
목표
판자로 막다
자동발사장치
자동발사장치

Issue

Does the law permit the use of a spring gun trap in an uninhabited dwelling to prevent unlawful entry by trespassers? 사람이 살지 않는

Holding and Reasoning

No. The owner of a premises may not willfully or intentionally injure a trespasser by means of deadly force, unless 토지, 부동산

the trespasser is endangering human life, committing a felony of violence, or committing a felony punishable by death. 위험하게 하다, 위해하다

Here, Katko's trespass posed no danger to human life, and it was not a felony of violence or one punishable by death. Such being the case, Briney's spring gun trap was unlawful and she is liable for Katko's injuries. One is not permitted to use deadly force against trespassers to a dwelling, unless the trespasser's intrusion poses a threat of death or serious bodily harm to the occupants therein. 상해

IV. Recapture of Chattels

The owner of chattel (personal property as opposed to real estate) may have several possible tort actions against one who interferes with use or possession of the chattel. The right to recover chattel involves a purely wrongful taking and conversion. If the possession is taken erroneously, the owner has no right to retake the chattel through use of personal force. The privilege to recapture chattel must be exercised promptly. 실수의

Diagram 10

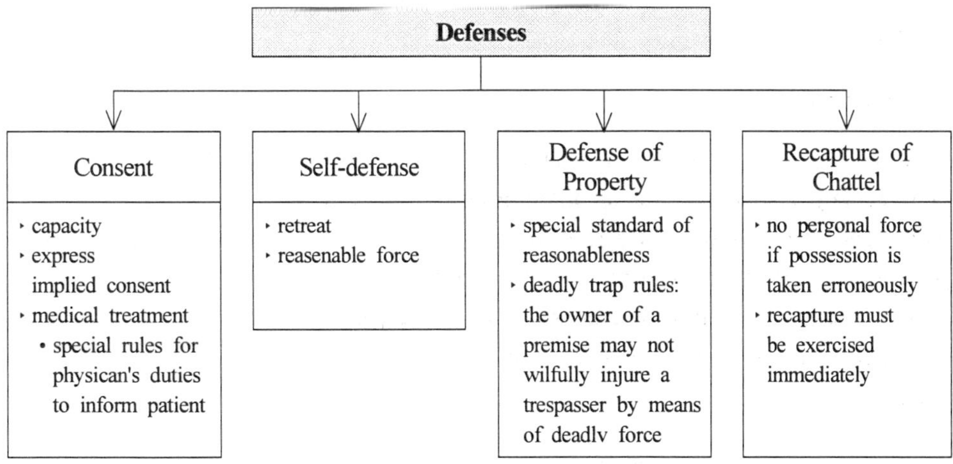

B. Intentional Torts Regarding Dignitary Injury

I. Defamation

Defamation is concerned with **injury to the reputation of another person.** The three following elements must be 명예훼손 / 명성, 신망

proven:

- the defendant made a defamatory statement concerning the plaintiff;
- the statement was published; and
- the statement damaged the plaintiff's reputation.

When the defamatory statement refers to a public figure, to establish a prima facie case two more elements are needed: 공인(公人)

- falsity of the defamatory language
- fault on defendant's part 책임

1. Defamatory language

Traditionally, words had a defamatory quality if they **exposed the plaintiff to hatred, ridicule, or contempt.** Defamatory statements also include anything that subjected the plaintiff to odium, shame, disgrace or other forms of discredit or harm to reputation. A publication is also defamatory if it causes the plaintiff to be shunned or avoided by others, even if he were not discredited or subjected to disgrace.

미움 / 조롱 / 경멸
악평, 오명 / 수치심 / 불명예
멀리하다 / 회피하다

2. Publication

Publication is a word of art. It includes **any communication, by any method to one or more persons who can understand the meaning.** Suggestive questions as well as declaratory statements can communicate defamatory meaning.

미술용어
암시적인, 도발적인 질문
선언적인 언명, 진술

A defamatory publication is actionable only by the person or persons to whom recipients reasonably or correctly believe it refers.

3. Damage to Plaintiff's Reputation

Regarding the damage to the plaintiff's reputation it is necessary to distinguish between libel and slander:

문서(로써 행한) 비방죄 / 구두(로 행한) 명예훼손

a) Libel

Libel is a defamatory statement **recorded in writing** or 기록하다

some other permanent from. General damages are presumed by law for all libels; i.e., special damages need not be established.

b) Slander

Slander is spoken defamation. It is compared to libel in a less permanent and less physical form. In slander, injury in **reputation** is not presumed. Thus, ordinary slander is not actionable in the absence of pleading and proof of special damages.

영속성이 적음
추정하다

4. Defenses

There are mainly three different kinds of defenses for torts regarding someone's dignity:

a) Absolute Privilege

Absolute privilege protects the speaker who is carrying out certain important duties, regardless of that person's motive or the truth or falsity of the statement. Absolute privilege usually arises from **involvement in judicial or legislative proceedings**, or by virtue of being a high-level governmental official.

중요한 의무
발생하다
~에 근거하여, ~로 인하여

An important special privilege that affects the media is the privilege of fair reporting an official action or proceeding, or of meetings open to the public that deal with matters of public concern.

언론의 보도특권

b) Qualified privilege

"Qualified privilege" may also be a defense to defamation. Qualified privilege is qualified in that it will not defeat a defamation claim if the defendant claiming it made the defamatory statement with actual malice, recklessness, or knowledge of falsity. Qualified privilege applies to communication related to a matter of public interest or where it is necessary to protect one's own interest.

악의 / 무모함, 전혀 배려가 없음

c) Truth

A defamatory statement must be false to be actionable.

But the **common law has considered truth to be a defense to defamation** rather than an element of the plaintiff's case. Thus, the defendant has the burden of proving the statement was true rather than the plaintiff having to prove that it was false. 입증책임

II. Invasion of Right to Privacy

Intrusive invasion of privacy includes many different protected areas: personality, solitude, private facts etc. Therefore, one can distinguish mainly four groups: 인격 / 홀로 거함, 독거 / 개인적 사실

- **appropriation** by defendant of plaintiff's picture or name for defendant's commercial advantage 사용, 전용, 도용
- **intrusion upon seclusion** 침해, 침입 / 은둔생활, 독거
- **false light**
- **public disclosure of private facts**

1. Appropriation

A prima facie case requires that the plaintiff proves an unauthorized use by defendant or plaintiff's picture or name for defendant's commercial advantage. 상업적 이익

2. Intrusion on Plaintiff's Seclusion

If the plaintiff wants to establish a prima facie case for invasion of privacy he must prove the following three elements:

- act of prying or intruding on the affairs of the seclusion of the plaintiff by the defendant 엿보다 / 침입하다
- the intrusion would be objectionable for a reasonable person 비난할 만한
- the thing to which there is an intrusion is private.

3. False Light

Displaying in a false light occurs when the plaintiff is placed before the public in a way that would be offensive to a reasonable person. False light cases are similar to defamation cases. However, recovery for being displayed in a false light does not require that it be proven that the portrayal would injure a person's reputation, as is the case with defamation.

보상, 회복
묘사, 기술

4. Public Disclosure of Private Facts

The plaintiff establishes a prima facie case of public disclosure of private facts if he can prove the following elements:

- ▶ publication by defendant of private information about the plaintiff
- ▶ the matter made public is such that a reasonable person would object to having it made public

Diagram 11

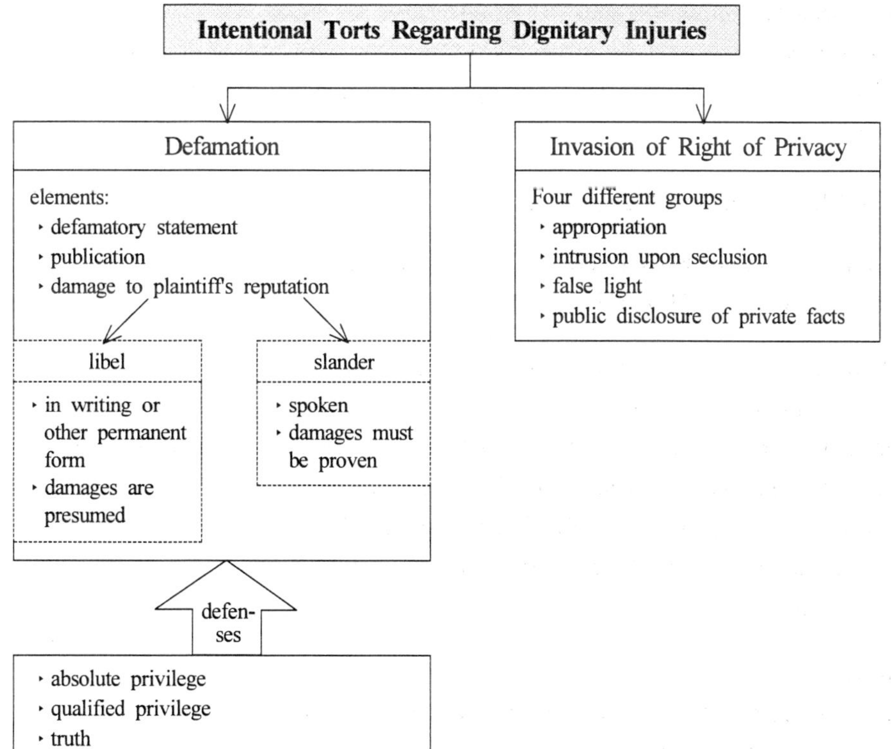

Part 2: Negligence

Besides intentional torts the common law has developed a system of negligence.

A person who negligently causes personal injury or property damage is subject to liability in tort. The following elements must be proved to establish a prima facie case:

- a **duty of reasonable care** 적절한 주의
- breach of that duty 위반
- causation
- resulting damages

A. Duty of Care

A general duty of care is imposed on all human activity. When a person engages in an activity, he is generally under the legal duty to act as an ordinary, **prudent and reasonable person.**

~을 행하다
신중한

I. Palsgraf v. Long Island Railroad Co.

Palsgraf v. Long Island Railroad Co. – Ct. of App. of New York, 248 NY 339 (1928)

A passenger (not the plaintiff) was running along the station platform to catch one of defendant's trains. Defendant's employees, in their efforts to help him, dislodged a package of fireworks from his arms. The packages fell on the tracks and exploded violently, causing some railroad scales at the other end of the platform to fall upon plaintiff and injure her.

제거하다, 떼어내다
안내판

Issue

Is a defendant liable for harm which his actions may cause to an unforeseeable plaintiff?

Holding and Reasoning

No. In his opinion, the renowned Judge Cardozo clearly

indicated that defendant's conduct was not a wrong towards the unforeseen plaintiff merely because the same conduct was a wrong (or an act of negligence) towards someone else. 예측하지 못한

The conduct of the defendant's guard, if a wrong in its relation to the holder of the package, was not a wrong in its relation to the plaintiff, standing far away. Relatively to her it was not negligence at all. Nothing in the situation gave notice that the falling package had in it the potency of peril to persons thus removed. Negligence is not actionable unless it involves the invasion of a legally protected interest, the violation of a right. The plaintiff as she stood upon the platform of the station might claim to be protected against intentional invasion of her bodily security. Such invasion is not charged. She might claim to be protected against unintentional invasion by conduct involving in the thought of reasonable man an unreasonable hazard that such invasion would ensue. These, from the point of view of the law, were the bounds of her immunity, with perhaps some rare exceptions, survivals for the most part of ancient forms of liability, where conduct is held to be at the peril of the actor. ... If no hazard was apparent to the eye of ordinary vigilance, an act innocent and harmless, at least to outward seeming, with reference to her, did not take to itself the quality of a tort because it happened to be a wrong, though apparently not one involving the risk of bodily insecurity, with reference to some one else.

힘, 잠재력
기소 가능한
법적으로 보호받는 이익
위험
뒤잇다
명백한 / 소심, 주의
불안정, 위험

The argument for the plaintiff is built upon the shifting meanings of such words as "wrong" and "wrongful," and shares their instability. What the plaintiff must show is "a wrong" to herself, i.e., a violation of her own right, and not merely a wrong to some one else, nor conduct "wrongful" because unsocial, but not "a wrong" to any one. Wrong is defined in terms of the natural or probable, at least when unintentional. ... The range of reasonable apprehension is at times a question for the court, and at times, if varying inferences are possible, a question for the jury. Here, by concession, there was nothing in the situation to suggest to the most cautious mind that the parcel wrapped in newspaper would spread wreckage through the station. If the guard had

범위, 영역
허가, 허락
잔해, 파편

thrown it down knowingly and willfully, he would not have threatened the plaintiff's safety, so far as appearances could warn him. His conduct would not have involved, even then, an unreasonable probability for invasion of her bodily security. Liability can be no greater where the act is inadvertent. — 고의가 아닌, 과실의

Negligence, like risk, is thus a term or relation. Negligence in the abstract, apart from things related, is surely not a tort, if indeed it is understandable at all. ... Negligence is not a tort unless it results in the commission of a wrong, and the commission of a wrong imports the violation of a right, in this case, we are told, the right to be protected against interference with one's bodily security. But bodily security is protected, not against all forms of interference or aggression, but only against some. One who seeks redress at law does not make out a cause of action by showing without more that there has been damage to his person. If the harm was not willful, he must show that the act as to him had possibilities of danger so many and apparent as to entitle him to be protected against the doing of it though the harm was unintended. — 보상, 배상

Judge Andrews dissented

In short, defendant owes a duty of care to anyone who suffers injuries as a proximate result of his breach of duty to someone.

According to this decision the reasonable person considers

- foreseeable risks of injury, — 예측가능한 위험
- the extent of the risk proposed by their conduct,
- the likelihood of the risk actually causing harm, — 개연성
- and whether alternatives to the proposed conduct would achieve the same purpose with a lesser or greater risk.

II. Custom

Custom is the way a certain activity is habitually carried out in a trade or a community. Custom is also a consideration. The fact that the conduct is generally engaged in by a — 관습, 관계 / 통상, 습관적으로

particular trade or profession **at least suggests that the conduct is acceptable.**

In some circumstances, reasonableness and custom diverge dramatically. Often the battle is which custom to use- a local standard or a national standard.

III. Statutory Standard of Care

The statutory standard of care prevails over the reasonable and prudent person because it sets the standard of care for a reasonable and prudent person, so if you break it you are not acting as a reasonable and prudent person.

우세하다(여기서는 <기준이> 더 높다)

Wright v. Brown — 356 A.2d 176 (1975)

Plaintiff Wright was attacked and injured by a dog belonging to defendant Brown. The dog had attacked another individual less than two weeks earlier, and had been placed in quarantine; the dog warden however, had released the dog prior to the expiration of the fourteen day quarantine period required by statute which sought to protect persons from being bitten by "diseased dogs." Wright brought suit against Brown, as well as against the town and the warden alleging that the warden was negligent in releasing the dog prior to the quarantine period prescribed by law. The trial court dismissed the claim against the town and the warden. The court reasoned that Wright was not within the class of persons which the statute sought to protect, since she had not alleged that she was bitten by a "diseased dog." Wright appealed.

검역소, (검역) 격리상태 / 관리인, 주인
경과
주장하다
기각하다
항소하다

Issue

Does one have an action for negligence when he incurs injury as a result of conduct proscribed by statute, if the injury is a type against which the statute was intended to protect?

Holding and Reasoning

Yes. Here, the dog quarantine statute was intended to protect persons bitten by a dog from the threat of rabies, as

광견병

well as to protect others from exposure to diseased dogs. In order to recover under a statute designed to protect persons from injury, one who is injured as a result of a violation of the statute must prove that he is in the class of persons protected by the statute, and must furthermore sustain the type of injury which the statute seeks to obviate. One intention of the statute at issue here was the protection of the general public. Since Wright is obviously a member of this class, her claim cannot be dismissed under the reasoning that she is not. She must still establish, however, that she sustained an injury of the type which the statute seeks to prevent. Reversed and remanded.

입증하다, 증명하다

증명하다, 설명하다

Where a statute is designed to protect persons against injury, one who has, as a result of its violation, suffered a type of injury which the statute was intended to avoid, has a cause of action for negligence.

고통받다

IV. The Relevance of Personal "Circumstances"

No allowance is made for a circumstance where a person lacks good judgment, is hasty or awkward because it would erupt in far too many standards for negligence. To narrow the test by focusing on circumstances rather than individual character and intelligence allows for a more objective test.

허락, 허용
곤란한

1. Disability

A person with a disability is held to a **reasonable standard for a person with a disability.**

Fletcher v. City of Aberdeen — 338 P2d 743 (1959)

Plaintiff is a blind man who was using his cane to walk down the street in the vicinity of some city construction. A city worker had posted barricades around the construction, but later removed them for ease of work and never replaced them. Plaintiff was injured as a result of not encountering any barricades to protect him from the construction.

지팡이
근처, 주변
만나다

Trial court found for plaintiff. The defendant appealed contending error in the jury instructions for refusal to instruct

주장하다

as they requested that the city did not have a higher degree of care required just because the plaintiff was blind.

Issue

Does the city have a higher degree of care towards disabled people?

Holding and Reasoning

Yes. The city is required to provide protection to a degree that would give a disabled person notice of the dangers to be encountered.

A person is required to use the degree of protection which would bring notice of the possible dangers to any potential victim who might be physically afflicted and therefore unable to exercise care on his own behalf. 피해자

The city should have known that blind persons were likely to use the street, and that their only reasonable means of avoiding obstacles was by use of a cane. Thus, the city was negligent in not providing a barricade for a blind person to warn him of the dangers he could not see. 장애물

2. Mental Illness

Courts hold the mentally ill person to the same standard as a mentally able person if the mentally ill person knows that insanity could occur.

Breunig v. American Family Insurance Co. – 173 N.W. 2d 619 (1970)

Erma Veith was insured against automobile accidents by the defendant, American Family Insurance Co. While driving on a road, Veith came under the sudden influence of insane delusions. Veith then entered an improper lane of traffic, colliding with a vehicle operated by the plaintiff Breunig. Breunig brought this action against Veith and her insurance company, and Veith's defense was that her sudden mental delusion rendered her incapable of operating her vehicle. A jury found that Veith had forewarning that her delusion might occur, and awarded a judgment to Breunig accordingly. 병적인 환상 사전경고

American Family Insurance Company appealed.

Issue
Is one liable in negligence for harm which he causes while insane?

Holding and Reasoning
Yes, if he had forewarning that a period of insanity might occur. Mental disability will not excuse an otherwise negligent act, if one had knowledge or warning that the disability might occur, and that it might cause him to suddenly lose control of his abilities. Insanity is generally a defense to torts which do not involve intent, and this rests on the principle that it is unjust to hold a person responsible for conduct which he is incapable of avoiding, and of which he had no forewarning. Conversely however, insanity is not a defense where as here one acts negligently while insane, having had knowledge of a condition which might bring on a period of insanity.

정신병, 정신적 장애

반대로

Where insanity occurs suddenly and without warning, the insane defendant is not held to the reasonable man standard.

3. Children

Children are held to a **different standard** but this does not mean they cannot be found negligent. When they are doing an **adult activity** they can be held to an **adult standard.**

a) General

Rudes v. Gottschalk – 324 SW2d 201 (TX 1959)

The plaintiff Gottschalk, an eight-year-old boy, was struck by a vehicle driven by defendant Rudes as he tried to cross an expressway. Since a statute was in existence which required pedestrians to yield the right of way except while crossing a road in a crosswalk, the trial court held that Gottschalk was guilty of negligence per se and denied him any recovery. Rudes appealed.

우선권을 주다

Issue

Should the conduct of a child be judged by the adult standard of care where statutory negligence is involved as opposed to common-law negligence? 판단하다

Holding and Reasoning

No. Where common-law negligence is involved, children are of course judged by the standard of care of a child as opposed to an adult. Here however, a statute existed which established a standard of conduct. This statute is adopted as the test for negligence here over the common-law ordinarily prudent man test, since the legislature is better positioned to establish tests of negligence than the courts. 행동의 준칙 입법자

However simply because such statutory negligence is involved does not require that a child's conduct be judged by an adult standard. Indeed, the overwhelming weight of authority in this country supports having the child standard of conduct applied in such situations.

Where negligence per se is involved, a child's conduct will be judged using the child standard of care as opposed to the adult standard. (실제책임의 유무와 무관한) 당연과실책임

b) Adult activities

But note the difference if children engage in adult activities.

Robinson v. Lindsey — 598 P.2d 392 (1978)

Plaintiff Robinson was a passenger on a snowmobile driven by defendant Anderson, and lost the use of a thumb when the vehicle was involved in an accident. At the time of the accident, Robinson was 11 years of age and Anderson was 13 years of age. Robinson brought suit against Anderson for her injuries, however the jury rendered a verdict in favor of Anderson. The trial court ordered a new trial, since it had instructed the jury as to the standard of care applicable to adults instead of that applicable to minors. 엄지손가락 미성년자

Issue

Should a minor be held to the adult standard of care while

operating a motor vehicle or while engaging in inherently dangerous activities? 원래, 그 자체로, 속성상

Holding and Reasoning

Yes. Traditionally, a flexible standard of care has been used to determine if a child's actions were negligent. The courts have evolved a special standard of care to measure the negligence of children, and this standard requires that a child's conduct be judged against that of a reasonably careful child of the same age, intelligence, maturity, training, and experience. A special exception has sometimes been created, however, for situations in which children are involved in certain dangerous activities. The most well-reasoned approach is that when a child engages in an inherently dangerous activity, such as the operation of a powerful motorized vehicle, he should be held to an adult standard of care. This will protect the need of children to be themselves, while also discouraging immature individuals from engaging in inherently dangerous activities. The operation of a snowmobile requires adult care and competence. Since Anderson was operating a powerful motorized vehicle in this case, he should be held to the standard of care and conduct expected of an adult.

과실의

성숙(함)

접근법

용기를 빼앗다, 곤란하게 하다 / 미성숙한

A minor is held to an adult standard of care while he operates powerful motorized vehicles or engages in inherently dangerous activities.

V. The Relevance of External Circumstances

Reasonableness of the decision must always be decided in relation to the unique context in which the person acted, e.g. the fact that the defendant must act quickly is relevant.

Wilson v. Sibert – 535 P.2d 1034 (1975)

The defendant Sibert was in his car and stationary in line at the drive-in window of a bank, and Wilson was stationary in her car behind him. A car in front of Sibert's began to back up, and Sibert, without checking to determine whether anything was behind him, immediately placed his car in

정지해 있는, 서있는

reverse motion. Sibert collided with Wilson's car, damaging and immobilizing it. The trial court gave instructions to the jury on negligence, as well as instructions on the "sudden emergency" doctrine, over Wilson's objection to the latter. The trial court also denied Wilson's motion for directed verdict on the issue of liability. Wilson appeals from a verdict against her.

후진 동작
이의

Issue

Is one who is confronted with an emergency held to the same standard of care toward others as when no emergency exists?

Holding and Reasoning

No. The law requires a jury to weigh the conduct of one charged with negligence against the standard of conduct of a reasonable person in the same circumstances. Thus an individual who is confronted with an emergency is not held to the standard of conduct normally applied to one who is not in an emergency situation. When circumstances include the presence of an emergency, such may render acceptable conduct which would be unreasonable absent an emergency. Here, Sibert was faced with a split-second decision. Since reasonable minds could differ as to the propriety of his actions, a directed verdict would not have been appropriate; thus the matter was properly submitted to the jury. Although Wilson asserts that the separate instruction on the emergency doctrine was prejudicial, it is predominantly accepted that it is not prejudicial error for a trial court to give a "superfluous" sudden emergency instruction.

행동의 표준, 행위준칙
긴급상황
적당, 타당함
적절한
편파적인 / 우세하게, 지배적으로

One who is faced with an emergency is charged with the level of care which would be exercised by a reasonable person confronted with the same emergency.

VI. Occupiers of Land

If someone occupies or enters another's land it is not easy to define the duty owed to the entering person.

1. Trespassers

As a general rule, the **landowner owes no duty to a trespasser** to make his land safe, to warn of dangers on it, to avoid carrying on dangerous activities on it, or to protect the trespasser in any other way. 점유침해자

The owner owes a duty of reasonable care to a **trespassing child** if:

- the owner knows that the area is one where children are likely to trespass; ~하기 쉬운, 개연성 있는
- the owner has reason to know that the condition poses an unreasonable risk of serious injury or death to trespassing children;
- the injured child either does not discover the condition or does not realize the danger, due to his youth; 발견하다
- the benefit to the owner of maintaining the condition in its dangerous form is slight weighed against the risk to the children; and
- the owner fails to use reasonable care to eliminate the danger.

2. Licensees

A licensee is a person who has the owner's consent to be on the property, but **who does not have a business purpose for being there,** or anything else entitling him to be on the land apart from the owner's consent. The main class of persons who qualify as licensees are "social guests." 허락받은 자 / 권한을 주다

The owner does not owe a licensee any duty to inspect for unknown dangers. On the other hand, if the owner knows of a dangerous condition, he must warn the licensee of that danger. 조사하다

3. Invitees

The owner does owe an invitee a duty of reasonable **inspection to find hidden dangers.** Also, the owner must use reasonable care to take affirmative action to remedy a ~할 의무를 지다 / 고객, 손님 / 확인하는

dangerous condition.

The class of invitees today includes:

▸ persons who are invited by the owner onto the land to conduct business with the owner; and 비즈니스를 하다

▸ those who are invited as members of the public for purposes for which the land is held open to the public.

If the visitor's use of the premises goes beyond the business purpose or beyond the part of the premises held open to the public, that person will change from an invitee to a licensee. The owner owes an invitee the duty of reasonable care. In particular, a duty to inspect and to warn.

Diagram 12

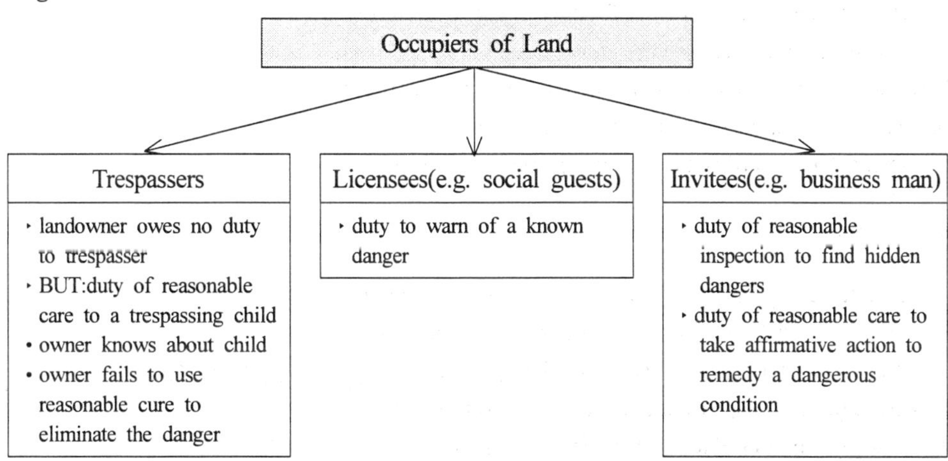

VII. Breach–Res Ipsa Loquitur

The plaintiff must show that the defendant failed to act with reasonable care, to behave as an ordinary prudent person would under like circumstances.

The doctrine of **res ipsa loquitur ("the thing speaks for itself")** allows the plaintiff to point to the fact of the accident, and to create an inference that, even without a precise showing of how the defendant behaved, the defendant was probably negligent. Courts generally impose **four requirements** for the res ipsa doctrine: 결론

- ▸ No direct evidence of the defendant's conduct 증거
- ▸ Seldom occurring without negligence
- ▸ Exclusive control of defendant
- ▸ Accident was not due to plaintiff's conduct

Usually, the effect of res ipsa is to permit an inference that the defendant was negligent, even though there is no direct evidence of negligence. Res ipsa thus allows a particular kind of circumstantial evidence. When res ipsa is used, the plaintiff has met his burden of production, and is thus entitled to go to the jury.

허락하다
설명책임

VIII. Causation

The plaintiff must show that the defendant's conduct was the "cause in fact" of the plaintiff's injury. The vast majority of the time, the way the plaintiff shows **"cause in fact"** is to show that the defendant's conduct was a **"but for" cause** of the plaintiff's injuries – had the defendant not acted negligently, the plaintiff's injuries would not have resulted.

1. Proximate Cause

Even after the plaintiff has shown that the defendant was the "cause in fact" of the plaintiff's injuries, the plaintiff must still show that the defendant was the "proximate cause" of those injuries. The **proximate cause requirement is a policy determination** that a defendant, even one who has behaved negligently, should not automatically be liable for all the consequences, no matter how improbable or far-reaching, of his act. Today, the proximate cause requirement usually means that the defendant will not be liable for consequences that are very unforeseeable.

직접적인 원인
결정
개연성이 없는

Gift v. Palmer – 141 A.2d 408 (Pa. 1958)

The three-year-old plaintiff Robert Gift was injured on a street in the city of Pittsburgh. There were no witnesses to his injury. Palmer was driving along the street on which the injured Gift was found, and testimony indicated that as Palmer proceeded down the street, he felt something hit his

증인
증언

front bumper. He continued along the street, until he noticed Gift lying in the street when he looked in his rear view mirror. Gift brought suit against Palmer for negligence, however the trial judge entered a nonsuit in favor of Palmer. Gift appealed.

범퍼
백미러

Issue

To recover for an accident, must a plaintiff prove by a preponderance of the evidence that the defendant was negligent and that his negligence was the proximate cause of the accident?

우세함

Holding and Reasoning

Yes. The mere happening of an accident is not evidence of negligence; negligence must be proven. Here, there were no eyewitnesses to the accident, and no evidence of the plaintiff's whereabouts just before the accident. There was no evidence showing that the only reasonable conclusion was that Palmer perceived Gift in a place of danger of an accident with his car, and that Palmer could have exercised reasonable care to avoid such an accident. In the absence of proof of negligence by the plaintiff, none may be found by the court.

목격자, 목격 증인
결론, 추론
증거

To prove negligence, a plaintiff must establish by a preponderance of the evidence that a defendant was negligent in his conduct, and that such negligence proximately caused the plaintiff's damages.

2. Intervening and Superseding Cause

Most proximate cause issues arise where the plaintiff's injury is precipitated by an "intervening cause." An intervening cause is a force which takes effect after defendant's negligence, and which contributes to that negligence in producing plaintiff's injury.

인과관계의 중단
힘, 세력
일조하다, 돕다

Some, but not all, intervening causes are sufficient to prevent defendant's negligence from being held to be the proximate cause of the injury. Intervening causes that are sufficient to prevent the defendant from being negligent are called "superseding" causes, since they supersede or cancel

인과관계의 추월, 추월적

defendant's liability. 인과관계

Generally courts use a foreseeability rule to determine whether a particular intervening cause is superseding. If the defendant should have foreseen the possibility that the intervening cause (or one like it) might occur, or if the kind of harm suffered by the plaintiff was foreseeable, defendant's conduct will nonetheless be the proximate cause. But if neither the intervening cause nor the kind of harm was foreseeable, the intervening cause will be a superseding one, relieving the defendant of liability.

IX. Defenses

A plaintiff who proves every element of a prima facie case for negligence will survive a directed verdict and get to the jury. Nevertheless, his recovery may be defeated or reduced if the defendant mounts a successful affirmative defense. In this part four types of defenses are examined: **contributory and comparative negligence, assumption of risk** and the **statute of limitations.**

지시평결, 지시된 평결*

행하다, 논하다 / 적극적 항변**

기여과실 / 비교과실

1. Contributory negligence

At common law, the doctrine of contributory negligence applies. The doctrine provides that a plaintiff who is negligent, and **whose negligence contributes proximately to his injuries,** is totally barred from recovery.

The plaintiff is held to the same standard of care as the defendant (i.e., the care of a "reasonable person under like circumstances").

The contributory negligence defense only applies where plaintiff's negligence contributes proximately to his injuries. The same test for "proximate causation" is used as where defendant's liability is being evaluated.

The doctrine of "last clear chance" acts as a limit on the contributory negligence defense. If, just before the accident,

---

* 배심에게 특정한 평결을 요구하는 판사의 지시, 지시에 따른 평결, 이는 보통 일방 당사자가 입증 책임을 다하지 못한 경우에 행해진다.

** 단순한 부인이 아니라, 새로운 사실을 적극적으로 제출하며 행하는 방어수단

the defendant had an opportunity to prevent the harm, and the plaintiff did not have such an opportunity, the existence of this opportunity (the last clear chance) wipes out the effect of plaintiff's contributory negligence.

기회 / 막다
없애다, 무찌르다

Chaffin v. Brame – 64 S.E.2d 276 (N.C. 1951)

While proceeding along a highway at night at about 40 miles per hour, the plaintiff Chaffin was approached by a vehicle driven by Garland, who was traveling in the opposite direction. Chaffin was temporarily blinded due to Garland's refusal to dim his headlights, and he collided with a truck owned by the defendant Brame. Brame's truck had been left on the highway, unlighted and blocking the entire right lane. Chaffin sued Brame for negligence, however Brame argued that Chaffin was guilty of contributory negligence. Brame's argument was that Chaffin had a duty to drive his vehicle at a speed which would allow him to stop within the distance that objects ahead could be seen. The trial court permitted the case to go to the jury, which found in Chaffin's favor. Brame appealed.

전조등
우측 차로

Issue

Is one guilty of contributory negligence if he strikes an obstruction, which is neither lit nor visible from light sources, while driving a motor vehicle upon a highway at night?

불을 밝힌 / 보이는

Holding and Reasoning

No. A person must exercise ordinary care to avoid injury when he drives a motor vehicle upon a highway at night. However this rule does not require the night driver to be perfect, and it will not preclude recovery when he collides with an unlighted obstruction, the presence of which is not apparent by available lights. Each case is judged on its own merits, however the ultimate inquiry concerns what a reasonably prudent person would have done under the same circumstances. Here, Chaffin was driving at a reasonable speed, and was keeping a proper lookout; upon becoming

배제하다
명백한, 보이는
정황

blinded by Garland's lights, he slowed his vehicle, proceeded with caution, and did all that was possible to avoid colliding with Brame's vehicle once it came into view. Accordingly, Chaffin was not contributorily negligent as matter of law.

2. Comparative negligence

A "comparative negligence" system rejects the all-or-nothing approach of contributory negligence. It instead attempts to **divide liability between the plaintiff and the defendant in proportion to their relative degrees of fault.** The plaintiff is not barred from recovery by his contributory negligence, but his recovery is reduced by a proportion equal to the ratio between his own negligence and the total negligence contributing to the accident.

시도하다

배제하다

Forty-six states have adopted some form of comparative negligence. Only 13 states have adopted "pure" comparative negligence. The rest completely bar the plaintiff if his negligence is (depending on the state) "as great" as defendant's, or "greater" than defendant's.

3. Assumption of Risk (자발적) 위험인수

A plaintiff is said to have assumed the risk of certain harm if he has voluntarily consented to take his chances that harm will occur. Where such an assumption is shown, the plaintiff is, at common law, completely barred from recovery.

자발적으로

a) Express assumption of risk

If the plaintiff explicitly **agrees** with the defendant, **in advance** of any harm, that plaintiff will not hold the defendant liable for certain harm, the plaintiff is said to have "expressly" assumed the risk of that harm.

명시적으로

Public policy usually prohibits a waiver of liability for the defendant's willful and wanton or "gross" negligence, and for defendant's intentionally tortuous conduct.

금하다 / 포기
의도적인

b) Implied assumption of risk

Even if the plaintiff never makes an actual agreement with the defendant whereby the plaintiff assumes the risk, the plaintiff may be held to have assumed certain risks by his conduct. Here, the assumption of risk is said to be "implied."

4. Statute of Limitations

Another defense is the statute of limitations. The discovery of injury is decisive. If the plaintiff does not discover his injury until long after defendant's negligent act occurred, the statute of limitations may **start to run at the time of the negligent act,** or may instead not start to run until the **plaintiff discovered** (or ought to have discovered) the injury. 시효(의 항변)

Diagram 13

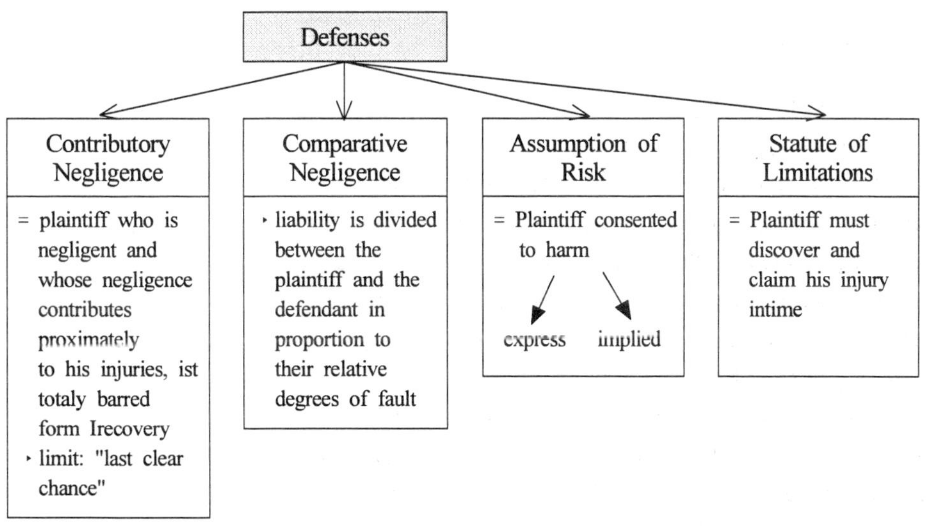

Part 3: Strict Liability

Strict liability is liability without fault. The defendant is subject to liability for conduct that amounts neither to negligence nor to any intentional tort. (채무를 진다는 의미의) 책임, 채무 / (유책하다는 의미의) 책임, 유책함

A. Abnormal Dangerous Activities

Strict liability is imposed on someone who engages in activities that are abnormally dangerous; characteristically those that are highly dangerous and that are not commonly pursued in the community.

I. The Old Concept

Rylands v. Fletcher – L.R. 3 H.L. 330 (1868)

The defendant retained an independent contractor to construct a pond in Lancaster, England. Beneath the land were the old mine shafts that had long since been filled or covered. Neither the contractor nor the landowner discovered any reason for concern. The ponded water eventually broke through the debris in the shafts and flowed into them, then through horizontal shafts to flood the plaintiff's mine.

위탁하다
연못
광산, 갱(坑)
파편, 잔해

Issue

Was the defendant strictly liable?

Holding and Reasoning

Yes. When a person who lawfully builds a water reservoir on his land, and the water thereafter escapes and does damage to another's property, the person is strictly liable for the damage caused by the escaped water.

If a person uses his land for any "non-natural" purpose of storing water, and the water escapes and does damage to another's property, then he is liable.

The damage would not have happened had the defendant not brought the water onto his land. In addition, the defendant should have known that if the water were to escape, it could cause damage. There was no implied consent under these circumstances because the plaintiff had no knowledge or control over how the defendant would use his land. Therefore the defendant would be liable unless the occurrence was an Act of God.

고도의 자연력

II. Later Developments

Courts now have generally accepted the principle that for some activities involving special dangers, especially those not commonly pursued, **liability** can be imposed **without fault**, often adopting the Restatement's formulation (Restatement 2nd, §520) according to which strict liability is more likely to be imposed if the defendant's activity

▶ creates a high risk
▶ with a likelihood of great harm 개연성
▶ that cannot be avoided by reasonable care, and if
▶ the activity is common and
▶ inappropriate at the particular site 부적절함

1. Explosives and high energy activities

Strict liability seems most readily imposed when physical harm results from the defendant's use or storage of dynamite or other materials intended to cause explosion. 저장

2. Poisons and other toxic material

Strict liability for abnormally dangerous activities has been imposed when the defendant has used toxic materials commercially to kill pests or protect crops. 유독성 해충 / 수확

B. Product Liability

The law of product liability is the area of law which deals with the liability of the manufacturer, wholesaler or retailer of a product for injuries resulting from dangerous and defective products. Products subject to the law run the spectrum from food, drugs, appliances, automobiles, medical devices, blood, tobacco, or even commercial jets. At common law the sale of a product was viewed as a commercial transaction upon which only the parties to the commercial contract could sue. The law has evolved to the point where today virtually anyone injured by a "defective" product can bring an action for damages against any party in the distributive chain of the product, whether it be the manufacturer, the wholesaler, the retailer or even the maker of a component part.

생산자 / 도매상 / 소매상
하자있는
가사기구
유통체인
부품공급자

1. General rule

Nearly all states apply the doctrine of **"strict product liability."** Most have based their approach on Restatement Second §402A. The basic rule is that a seller of a product is liable without fault for personal injuries (or other physical harm) caused by the product if the product is sold:

(1) in a **defective** condition that is
(2) **unreasonably dangerous** to the user or consumer.

Once these requirements are satisfied, the seller is liable even though he used all possible care, and even though the plaintiff did not buy the product from or have any contractual relationship with the seller.

Strict product liability applies not only to the product's manufacturer, but also to its retailer, and any other person in the distributive train (e.g., a wholesaler) who is in the business of selling such products.

II. Defective

A product meets these twin requirements of "defective" and "unreasonably dangerous" if it is "dangerous to an extent beyond that which would be contemplated by the ordinary consumer who purchases it, with the ordinary knowledge common to the community as to its characteristics."

이중의, 쌍둥이의

1. Unavoidably unsafe products

A product will not give rise to strict liability if it is unavoidably unsafe, and its **benefits outweigh its dangers.**

이익, 장점, 유리한 점

2. Measured by time of sale

Generally, "unreasonable danger" and "defectiveness" are measured by reference to the state of human knowledge at the time the product was sold, not the time the products liability case comes to trial. In other words, if the manufacturer did not and could not reasonably have known of the danger at the time of manufacture, it will not be strictly liable. This is often called the **"state of the art" defense.**

~와 관련하여

선행기술, 기존의 기술수준

3. Obvious dangers

If the danger posed by a product is very obvious or

commonly known to consumers in general, the product will generally be found not to be defective or unreasonably dangerous.

For instance, a court would almost certainly hold that although cigarettes are dangerous, the dangers they pose are so obvious and well known that a cigarette manufacturer cannot be held strictly liable for making an unreasonably dangerous or defective product. 명백한

III. Design Defects

A "design defect" must be distinguished from a "manufacturing defect." In a design defect case, all the similar products manufactured by the defendant are the same, and they **all bear a feature whose design is itself defective,** and unreasonably dangerous. 구별하다 특징

1. Negligence predominates

Most design defect claims have a heavy negligence aspect, even though the complaint claims strict liability. A design defect claim requires the plaintiff to show that the defendant chose a design that posed an unreasonable danger to the plaintiff. The defectiveness of a design is judged by comparing it to other possible designs. A product's design will be deemed defective if two conditions are met:

- ▸ there was a feasible alternative design which, consistent with the consumer's expected use of the product, would have avoided the particular injuries; and 실행가능한
- ▸ the costs of the alternative design are less than the costs of the injuries thereby avoidable.

2. Suitability for unintended uses

The defendant may be liable not only for injuries occurring when the product is used as intended, but also for some types of injury stemming from unintended uses of the product. 유래하다

a) Unforeseeable misuse

If the misuse of the product is not reasonably foreseeable, the defendant has no duty to design the product so as to protect against this misuse. 예측가능한

b) Foreseeable misuse

But if the misuse is reasonably foreseeable by the defendant, he must take at least **reasonable design precautions to guard against the danger from that use.** (Alternatively, a warning to the purchaser against the misuse may sometimes suffice.) 예방책, 대비책 / 충분하다

IV. Warning

The "duty to warn" is essentially an extra obligation placed on a manufacturer.

1. Manufacturing defect

Thus if a product is defectively manufactured, no warning can save the defendant from strict liability.

2. Design defect

Similarly, if a product is defectively designed, a warning will generally not shield the defendant from strict product liability. 보호하다

3. Properly manufactured and designed product

If a product is properly designed and properly manufactured, the defendant must nonetheless give a warning if there is a non-obvious risk of personal injury from using the product. Similarly, in this situation, the defendant may be liable for not giving instructions concerning correct use, if a reasonable consumer might misuse the product in a foreseeable way.

Diagram 14

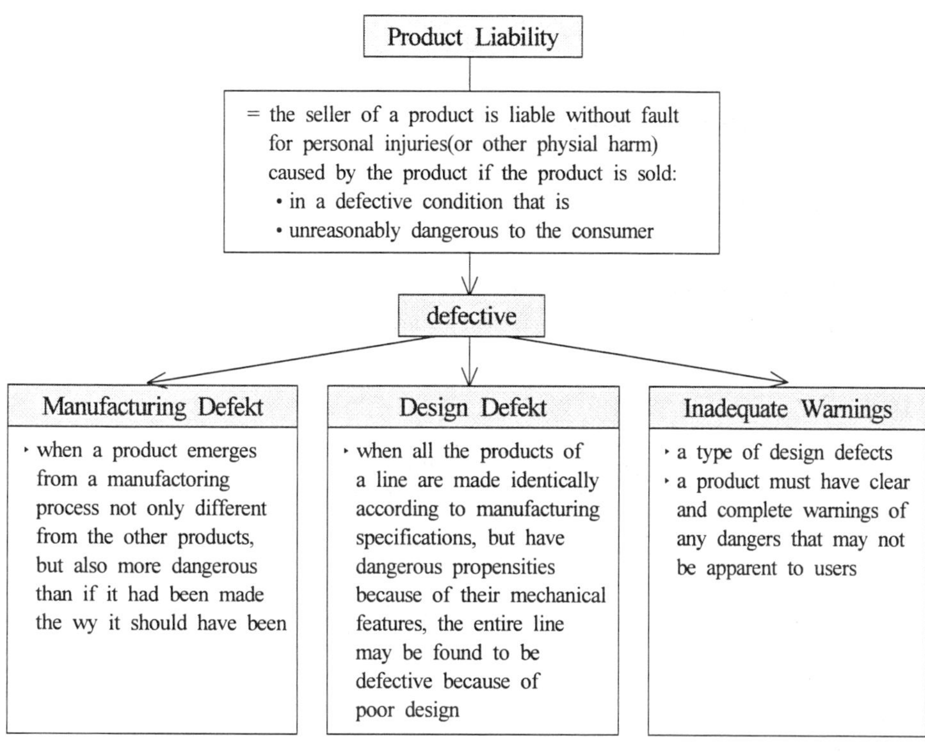

4. Latest developments

Sometimes, the duty to warn is taken too seriously. Thus, the warning can be as funny as follows:

▸ warning on a hairdryer: "Do not use while showering!"

▸ warning on a lawnmower: "Do not hold head under lawnmower". 잔디깎는 기계

▸ warning on a foil that is put behind a car's windshield to keep sun/heat out: "Remove before driving."

Further reading

Vetri, Tort Law and Practice (1998); *Shapo*, Tort and Injury Law (2nd ed., 2000); *Vandall/Wertheimer*, Torts: Cases and Problems (1997); *Diamond e.a.*, Understanding Torts (2nd ed.); *Prosser/Keeton*, On Torts (1984); *Harper/James/Gray*, The Law of Torts (1996); *Levmore*, Foundations of Tort Law (1993); *Rabin*, Perspectives on Tort Law (1990).

Chapter Six

Business Associations

Part 1: Doing Business

The following diagram gives an overview about the different ways of doing business in the United States:

Diagram 15

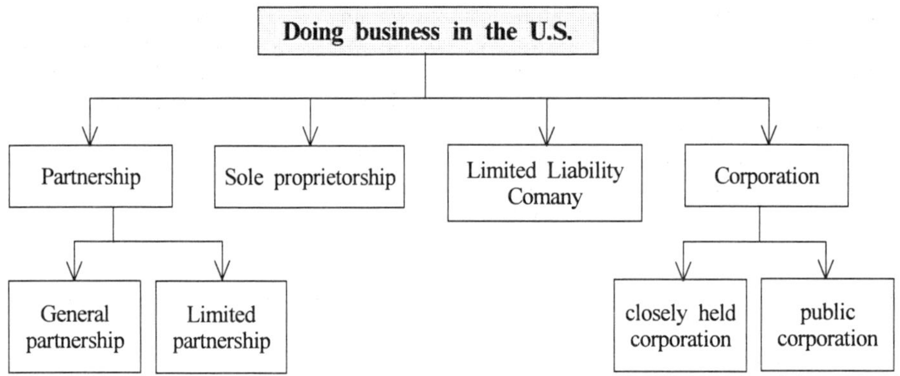

Part 2: Sole Proprietorship

A sole proprietorship is the **simplest form of business organization** which can be found under US law. This type of business organization is usually chosen by the one-person business, in which the owner and worker are the same person. Nevertheless sole proprietorships can have employees. A vast majority of the small businesses in the United States are operated as sole proprietorships. 개인기업 근로자

There are several advantages connected with this type of organization. Most important is that it is easy to form a sole proprietorship. On the other hand there are some disadvantages. It can have only one owner and the owner is individually responsible for all losses of the business. 장점 손실

A. Beginning of Operation

By beginning to operate a business a sole proprietorship can come to existence. It is usually operated under the name of the individual owner, but other names can also be used. Care should be taken in selecting a name to ensure it is not the same or similar to the name of another business.

There are many states prohibiting the use of the words "incorporated," "Inc.,", "Co." or something alike in combination with the name of a sole proprietorship unless the business is a corporation. 회사

B. Ownership

Owner of the sole proprietorship is the **person who creates it.** This person owns all the assets of the business. A sole proprietorship may be owned by only one individual. If two or more persons own a business, a partnership comes into existence. 재단, 자산 / 인적 결합회사(조합)

In a sole proprietorship, the business and the owner are one and the same. There is no separate legal entity and thus no separate legal "person." This means that a sole proprietor has unlimited personal responsibility for his business's liabilities. 법인격 / 채무, 책임

C. Continuity and Transferability

A sole proprietorship terminates with the death of the owner. It can exist as long as its owner is alive and desires to continue the business. The assets and liabilities of the business become part of the owner's estate. 끝나다 / 바라다 / 재산권

A sole proprietor can **freely transfer a business by selling all or a portion of the assets of the business.** 양도하다

Diagram 16

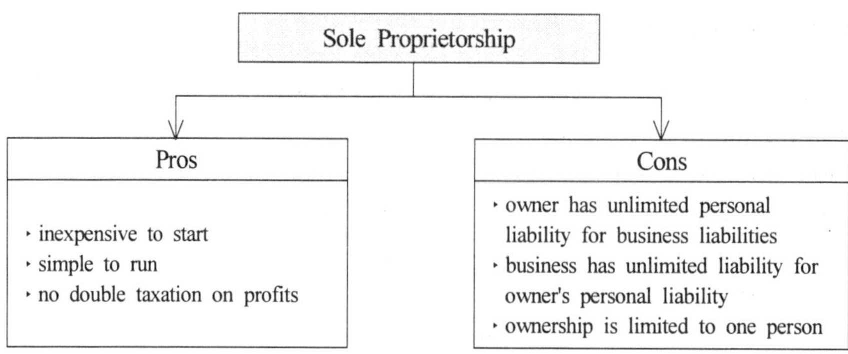

Part 3: Partnership

Generally, two types of partnerships can be distinguished. There is the basic form of a partnership, in which every member of the partnership has the same rights and duties including full liability. For the purpose of distinction in the following chapter this form of partnership will be called **"general" partnership.** Partnerships in which liabilities are limited will be called **"limited" partnerships.** The details of this limitation will be given later in this chapter.

구별

A. "General" Partnership

A "general" partnership is any association of two or more people who carry on a business as co-owners. A general partnership can come into existence by operation of law, with no formal papers signed or filed. Any partnership is a "general" one unless the special requirements for limited partnerships (see below) are complied with.

연결, 결합
법률에 의하여
요구사항

I. Applicable Law

Partnerships are governed by two sets of statutes: The **Uniform Partnership Act** ("UPA") and the **Revised Uniform Partnership Act** ("RUPA").

법률

Originally there was only the Uniform Partnership Act, which was promulgated by Commissioners on Uniform State Laws in 1914 and was adopted in every US State except

채용하다, 도입하다

Louisiana. In 1994 the Commissioners on Uniform State Laws promulgated the Revised Uniform Partnership Act, which is intended to supersede UPA. But since many states have not adopted the new rules yet, most cases are still based on UPA, and since a lot of RUPA regulations continue many of the rules of UPA, cases in this section will largely concern UPA.

공표하다
대체하다

Both of these statutes are default rules. They apply only if the partners have not agreed otherwise in a partnership agreement.

대체규정
인적회사계약

II. Formation

According to the UPA a Partnership is an **association of two or more persons to carry on as co-owners of a business for profit** (UPA §6). RUPA contains the same rule (RUPA §202).

이윤추구목적 사업

Therefore there are five critical elements to the existence of a partnership for purposes of partnership law. There must be

- ▶ An association
- ▶ Two or more persons
- ▶ A relationship formed to carry on a business
- ▶ A business for profit
- ▶ Co-owners of the business

1. Agreement

The rules applicable to contracts determine if there is an agreement which may create a partnership.

적용되는

a) Capacity

The basic rule is the same as that governing a principal in an **agency relationship.** Anyone may be a partner who is capable of entering into a binding contract.

(대리인에 대하여) 본인, 당사자
대리관계
~할 수 있는

If a would-be partner lacks capacity, he is not personally liable for the obligations of the partnership or for breaches of the partnership agreement. But he is bound to the extent of his contribution of capital to the partnership. 기여

b) Formalities

There are no particular formalities essential to the validity of a contract of partnership. In the absence of a statute, the partnership agreement may be either express or implied (i.e., established solely from the conduct of the parties). It is normally not necessary for the partnership agreement to be in writing. 요식행위, 형식

Partnership agreements that cannot be performed within **one year** must be in writing in order to satisfy the Statute of Frauds (see supra, vol. I, p. 150). 수행하다

c) Legality of Purpose

There must be a legal purpose for which the partnership is formed or is to be formed. The illegality of the business will make the partnership null and void. If there is an illegal purpose, a court will compel neither an accounting nor a settlement of the partnership affairs. 무효의 / 강제하다 / 회계, 부기

2. Partnership by Estoppel

In general a partnership comes to existence through an agreement, express or implied, between the parties. In certain situations, however, even though there is no agreement and the parties between themselves are not partners, they may nevertheless be held liable to third parties as if they were partners.

There are **two important types of partnerships by estoppel.**

a) Liability of Person Who Is Held Out as Partner

When a person, by words or conduct, **represents himself or permits another to represent him as a partner,** he will be liable to third parties who extend credit to the actual or apparent partnership on the faith of (i.e., in reliance on) the representation. 소개하다, 드러내다

b) Liability of Person Who Holds Another Out as Partner

When a person, by words or conduct, holds another person

out to be his partner, he thereby makes such alleged partner his agent with the power to bind him to third parties as if the other were, in fact, a partner. If the person making such representation is in fact a member of an already existing partnership and the representation is to the effect that the would-be partner is a member of this partnership, only those partners who made or consented to the representation will be bound.

주장하다(hier : 주장되는, 파트너라고 주장한 사람)

동의하다

Young v. Jones – 816 F. Sup. 1070 (1993)

The plaintiff, an investor from Texas, deposited $ 550,000 in a South Carolina bank on the basis of an unqualified audit letter issued by Price Waterhouse – Bahamas, the defendant, regarding the financial statement of Swiss American Fidelity and Insurance Guaranty (SAFIG). The letterhead used for the SAFIG audit identified the Bahamian accounting firm only as "Price Waterhouse", and the audit letter also bore a Price Waterhouse trademark and signature. The financial statement turned out to be falsified, and the plaintiff lost the deposited money. The plaintiff filed suit to recover the lost funds and investment potential alleging that the defendant knew that the letter would induce third parties to rely to their detriment on the financial statement. The plaintiff asserted that the defendant and Price Waterhouse – U.S. operated as a partnership, or in the alternative, operated as partners by estoppel, and therefore Price Waterhouse – U.S. should be held liable for the negligent acts of defendant. The defendant and Price Waterhouse – U.S. denied that a partnership existed between the two and submitted documents establishing that the two were separately organized.

(편지나 문서의) 머리부분(회사에 대한 정보가 포함된 부분)

상표

위조하다(hier : 위조된)

손해

금반언에 의한 회사원(파트너), 과실적 회사원

과실있는, 부주의한

부인하다

Issue

Is a person who represents himself, or permits another to represent him, to anyone as a partner in an existing partnership or with others not actual partners, liable to persons to whom such a representation is made who has given credit to the actual or apparent partnership?

<u>Holding and Reasoning</u>

Yes. A person who represents himself, or permits another to represent him, to anyone as a partner in an existing partnership or with others not actual partners, is liable to any such person to whom such a representation is made, and who has given credit to the actual or apparent partnership.

Although the plaintiff alleges that Price Waterhouse holds itself out as an international accounting firm, he can point to nothing concrete that should hold the various <u>affiliated entities</u> liable for the acts of others. There is no evidence that the plaintiff relied on any act or statement by any Price Waterhouse – U.S. partner indicating the existence of a partnership with defendant. Even if there were, there has been no evidence presented that any member of Price Waterhouse – U.S. had anything to do with SAFIG's falsified financial statement or any other act related to the lost investment. The <u>allegations</u> of negligence against defendant cannot serve to hold members of Price Waterhouse – U.S. liable as partners by estoppel.

자매회사

(hier : 과실이 있었다는) 주장

Diagram 17

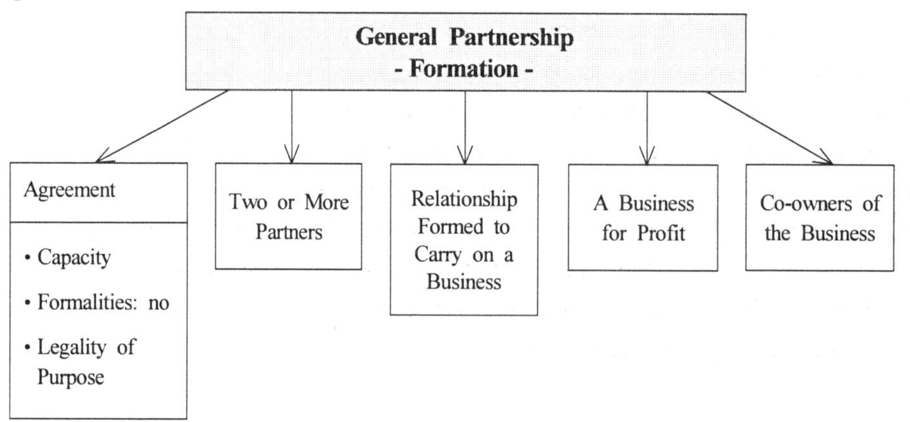

III. Relations Between Partners

The rights and duties regulating the relationship between partners of a partnership are determined by §18 of the UPA. The rule provides that partners have equal rights concerning the management of the partnership. Disputed issues are decided by majority.

1. Participation in Management

Absent an agreement to the contrary, all partners have equal rights in the management of the partnership business.

Summers v. Dooley – 481 P.2d 318 (1971).

This lawsuit involves a claim by one partner (Summers as plaintiff) against the other for $6,000. The complaining partner asserts that he has been required to pay out more than $11,000 in expenses without any reimbursement from either the partnership funds or his partner. 주장하다

The parties are partners in a trash collection business. Dooley became unable to work for the business. Although business was booming, Defendant Dooley refused to hire another employee to do his work. Plaintiff Summers hired an employee without permission of defendant Dooley and later demanded reimbursement from defendant Dooley for his expenditures. 쓰레기 수집회사 / 고용하다 / 동의, 허락

Issue

Whether an equal partner in a two-man partnership has the authority to hire a new employee over the objection of the other partner and then attempt to charge the dissenting partner with the costs incurred as a result of his unilateral decision? 이의 / 시도하다

Holding and Reasoning

Yes, there is the right to charge the opposing partner.

In the instant case the record indicates that although Summers requested that his partner Dooley agree to the hiring of a third man, such requests were not honoured. In fact Dooley made it clear that he was "voting no" with regard to the hiring of an additional employee.

An application of the relevant statutory provisions and pertinent case law to the factual situation presented by the instant case indicates that the trial court was correct in its 적절한, 꼭 들어맞는 / 시사하다, 보여주다

disposal of the issue since a majority of the partners did not consent to the hiring of the third man."

The court went on by saying that it was its opinion that the relevant statute was of a mandatory rather than permissive nature. — 의무적인, 구속력 있는 / 임의적인

Whether a statute is mandatory or directory does not depend upon its form, but upon the intention of the legislature, to be ascertained from a consideration of the entire act, its nature, its object, and the consequences that would result from construing it one way or the other. — 훈시적인 / 확정하다

The intent of the legislature may be implied from the language used, or inferred on grounds of policy or reasonableness. But in spite of the fact that one of the two partners refused to consent to the hiring of additional help, nonetheless, the non-consenting partner retained profits earned by the labor of the third man and therefore the non-consenting partner should be estopped from denying the need and value of the employee, and has by his behavior ratified the act of the other partner who hired the additional man. — 보유하다, 유지하다 / 금반언(estoppel)을 적용하여 금지하다

2. Remuneration

Partners are not entitled to any remuneration for services rendered to the partnership unless the partnership agreement provides to the contrary. This is the same even in cases where one partner is forced to assume more work than he had anticipated and the other partner does nothing to further the affairs of the partnership. However, where partners do not have an equal interest, are not equally liable, and are not equally responsible for the conduct of the partnership business, it is possible to infer an agreement to compensate a partner for extraordinary services. — 대가 / 동일한 지분 / 특별한, 통상적이지 않은

3. Indemnification

The partnership must indemnify every partner in respect of payments made and personal liabilities reasonably incurred by him in the ordinary and proper conduct of its business, or for the preservation of its business or property. — 면책해주다 / 보존, 보호

4. Contribution

In cases where one partner is compelled to pay or satisfy the whole or more than his share of a partnership debt, he may require (usually in an action in equity) the other partners to contribute their pro rata shares.

강제하다

비례하여, 몫에 해당하는 비율로

5. Fiduciary Duty

Each partner owes a fiduciary duty to the partnership. Each partner is bound to use the partnership property and exercise his partnership powers for the benefit of the partnership and not for himself alone. Profits made in the course of the partnership belong to the partnership, and one partner will not be permitted to gain for himself at the expense of the partnership.

수탁자로서의 의무

이익, 유리함

6. Information

The partnership books must be kept, subject to an agreement to the contrary, at the partnership's principal place of business and every partner has the right to inspect and copy them. Each partner, upon demand of another partner (or his legal representative) must "render true and full information of all things affecting the partnership."

본사 주소

허락하다

7. Legal Actions between Partners

a) General Rule

As a general rule, **a partner cannot sue or be sued by the partnership** (in an action at law), nor may one partner sue another partner on matters related to the partnership business.

b) Actions for an Accounting

An accounting is an equitable proceeding that considers all transactions between partners in connection with the partnership. It is usually held in connection with a final settlement of the partnership affairs. The liabilities between each partner and the partnership are thereby converted into liabilities between the partners individually.

회계

전환하다

IV. Relations of Partners to Third Parties

1. Authority

The authority of a partner to bind the partnership when dealing with third parties is governed by the law of agency. Every partner is an agent of the partnership for the purpose of its business. The act of every partner "for apparently carrying on in the usual way the business of the partnership" (within the scope of the partnership business) will bind the partnership and thereby bind other partners. Liability may be in contract, tort, or for breach of trust.

대리에 관한 법
대리인
배신(신뢰를 저버림)

a) Actual Authority

To determine whether a particular act was actually authorized, one must establish **whether the appropriate authorizing vote was cast.** This may be done in several ways.

(표를) 던지다, 결정하다

aa) Authorized by Agreement

An action by a particular partner may be authorized by the partnership agreement, in which case no further vote is necessary.

위임하다, 권능을 부여하다

bb) No Specific Authorization

In a case where the acting partner is not specifically authorized by the partnership agreement to do the particular act, then a **majority vote of the partners is required.** The vote can also authorize a partner to act in certain classes of transactions without further consultations with the other partners.

다수표결
자문

b) Apparent Authority

If there is no actual authority, a partner can under general agency principles bind the partnership because of his apparent authority. This is the case, when a **third party reasonably believes the agent has authority because of the principal's actions.**

명백한 대리권, 권능, 권한

But an act which is not apparently related to the partnership business is not within his apparent authority, and does not bind his co-partners, unless, it has been actually authorized by them. And if the third party had notice that the partner's acts were in violation of the partnership agreement, the other partners are not liable. 위반

2. Liability

a) Liability of Present Partners

Generally, partners who are member of the partnership at the time the claim is brought up they are liable for the amount of every debt of the partnership. In detail one must distinguish between the following forms of liability: 청구권

aa) Contract Liability 계약적 책임, 채무

Partners will be liable on contracts made by the partnership in the scope of the partnership business and on any other contracts expressly authorized by a partner. Each partner is liable for the whole amount of every debt of the partnership, not merely for a proportionate part. 비율에 따르는

Partners' contract liability is joint rather than several. There is no several liability in contract issues. This is made clear by the rule of the UPA §15 (b). The rules of the RUPA come to a different conclusion in these kind of questions. According to §307 of the RUPA all partners are jointly and severally liable for all obligations of the partnership. A typical consequence of joint liability is that in a lawsuit every partner of a partnership sued must be named. 공동의 / 단독의, 개별적인 의무 소송

bb) Tort Liability

Partners will be **jointly and severally liable for any torts committed by any partner** or by an employee of the partnership in the ordinary course of partnership business (UPA §15(a)). This liability will be extended to frauds committed by a co-partner in the course of transactions and business of the partnership, even though the other partners have no connection with, knowledge of, or participation in the fraud. 불법행위 범하다 사기, 기망

Because liability in torts is both joint and several, an action may be brought against any single partner without joining the others. (소를) 제기하다

b) Liability of an Incoming Partner

A person admitted as a partner into an existing partnership is **liable for all the obligations of the partnership arising before his admission** as though he had been a partner when such obligations were incurred. However, his liability shall be satisfied only out of partnership property.

(채무를) 지다
인적회사(=조합) 재산

c) Liability of a Retiring Partner

A retiring partner remains **liable on all obligations incurred by the partnership while a member of the partnership,** unless there has been payment, release, or novation. In general, he is liable for acts done until he has not only withdrawn from the partnership, but has also given notice of his withdrawal.

퇴사하는 회사원
경개
채무인수, 채무의 경개(更改)*
탈퇴하다, 퇴사하다

Diagram 18

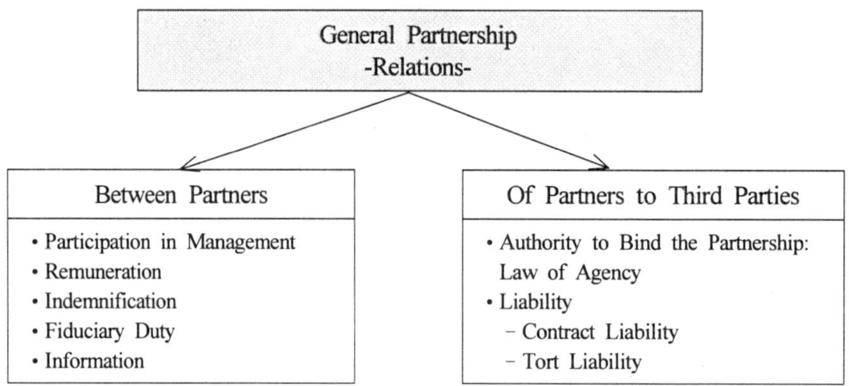

V. Dissolution

The UPA deals with different ways of dissolution in its §§29 ff.

해산

1. Types of dissolution

Dissolution is the "change in the relationship of the partners caused by any partner ceasing to be associated in the carrying on as distinguished from the winding up of the business." It is important to note that a **dissolution** is **simply**

폐업하다

* 기존채무를 새로운 채무로 대체하는 로마법상의 개념. 영미법의 실제에 있어서는 대개 채무자가 교체되는 경우만을 지칭하므로 채무인수(Schuldübernahme)라고 번역할 수 있다.

a change in legal relationship. It does not mean that the business has been ended or any assets have been distributed to partners. Dissolution may be caused in three ways: 재산

- by act of the parties;
- by operation of law; or
- by court decree.

a) Act of the Parties

A partnership contract may set a definite term to the partnership relationship, or it may set achievement of a particular undertaking as a purpose of the partnership. When that term has elapsed or the undertaking is accomplished, the partnership automatically terminates or dissolves. 달성, 성취, 성공 완수하다

A partnership may be brought to an end at any time by the **mutual assent** of all partners. 합의

b) Dissolution by Operation of Law

Any event that makes it unlawful for the business to be carried on will dissolve the partnership. 해산하다

Also the bankruptcy of any partner or the death of a partner will dissolve the partnership.

c) Dissolution by Decree

Upon the application of one or more of the partners, a court of equity may, for sufficient reason, decree the dissolution of a partnership. The following are sufficient reasons for a decree of dissolution: 판결을 내리다

- Breach of Partnership Agreement
- Unprofitability 수익성이 없음

2. Notice

Third parties who have dealt with the partnership and those who have simply known of the partnership prior to dissolution **are entitled to proper notice** published in newspapers of general circulation in the area in which the partnership carries on its business. Failure to furnish this information to such third parties will bind members of the 권한을 부여하다 전달하다, 공급하다

former partnership to such third parties who, while unaware of the dissolution, extend credit to the partnership.

Those who were creditors at the time of dissolution or who had extended credit to the partnership prior to dissolution are entitled to personal notice. It does not matter whether they have advanced a large or small amount or if there were only one or two transactions between the partnership and the third party. If, however, the third party has dealt with the partnership only on a cash basis and has never been a partnership creditor, he is only entitled to the notice that is given to the general public.

채권자

일반공중

3. Business Transactions After Dissolution

Principally, the dissolution of a partnership terminates the authority of any partner to act as an agent for either the partnership or the other partner, except for the purpose of winding up the affairs of the partnership. However, if the partnership agreement provides that the business is to be continued by one or more of the partners, the agreement controls and the business will be continued by the new partners without any winding up.

대리권, 권능

효력을 지니다

After dissolution, absent an agreement to the contrary, the **partnership must be wound up**. Authority exists to carry out the necessary acts. However, generally only transactions designed to terminate, rather than to carry on, the business are within the scope of the partner's actual authority. In short, “old business” can be wrapped up; if “new business” is entered into, the partner who continues on behalf of the partnership with knowledge of the dissolution assumes sole liability (unless partnership liability arises from failure to give notice as described above). If losses result, he alone will bear them.

반대의 약정이 없는 경우

전제하다, 수용하다

손실

4. Distribution of Assets

Where a solvent partnership is dissolved and its assets are reduced to cash, such cash shall be used to pay the partnership's liabilities in the following order:

▸ Outside Creditors
▸ Partners

Diagram 19

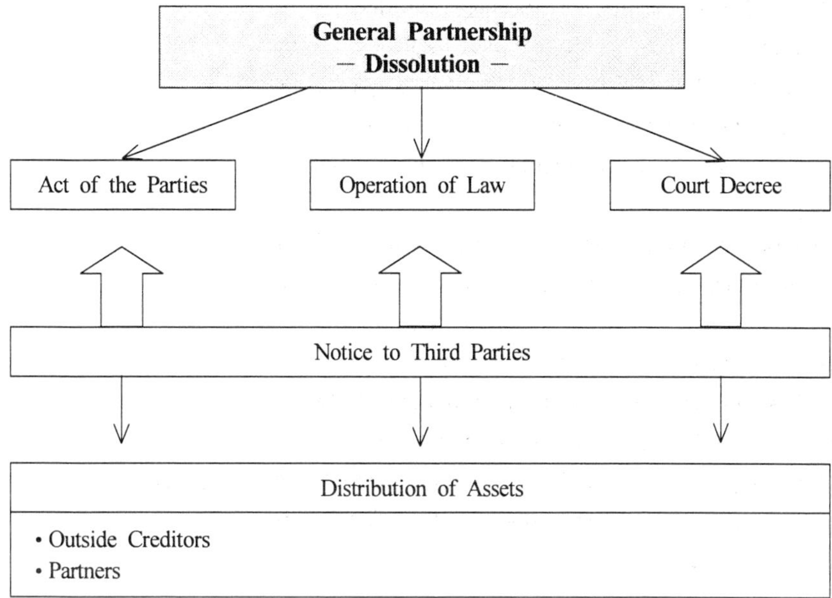

B. Limited Partnerships — 유한책임 인적회사(조합)

The limited partnership consists of two or more persons carrying on as co-owners of a business for profit. There are two types of partners. There is the **general partner** (유사개념) 무한책임사원 who has unlimited liability for all debts of the partnership as do the partners in a "general" partnership described above. Additionally, there must be at least one **limited partner** (유사개념) 유한책임사원 whose liability is limited.

1. Applicable Law

The applicable laws are the **Uniform Limited Partnership Act** ("ULPA") and the Revised Uniform Limited **Partnership** Act ("RULPA"). The first one was promulgated (공표하다) by the Commissioners on Uniform State Laws in 1916 and the latter in 1976. All States except Louisiana adopted (채용하다, 도입하다) the ULPA. The Commissioners' intention was that the RULPA should replace the older act. The RULPA has been widely, but not universally, adopted since 1976. Additionally, the Commissioners amended the Revised Uniform Limited Partnership Act in 1985. 개정하다, 보충하다

All these changes to the acts dealing with the law of limited partnerships have reflected the influence of the corporate model. This means that the limited partnership became more and more an entity which in some respects comes even closer to a corporation than to a "general" partnership. 영향력 독립된 법인격

Because of the different versions of acts dealing with the law of limited partnerships in many states and because of differences in terminology used by several state acts, in this part New York Law will be concentrated on.

New York adopted the Revised Uniform Limited Partnership Act ("R.U.L.P.A."), which became effective July 1, 1991. The act governs any limited partnership formed after July 1, 1991, and any existing partnership that elects to be governed by the act. 규율하다, 규정하다

II. Two Types of Partners

Limited partnerships have two types of partners

- one or more "general" partners, who are each **liable for all the debts** of the partnership; and
- one or more "limited" partners, who are **not liable** for the debts of the partnership **beyond the amount they have contributed.** 기여하다

III. Formation Requirements

In contrary to a "general" partnership a limited partnership can only be formed if certain formalities are complied with and certain filings are made. Factual characteristics of a relationship between two or more persons are not alone sufficient. 준수하다, 지키다 서류의 제출

To form a limited partnership in New York, a certificate of limited partnership must be executed and filed in the department of state. The certificate must set forth: 실행하다 (州의) 내무부

▸ the **name** of the limited partnership;
▸ the **county** in which the office of the limited partnership is to be located; 군(郡)
▸ a **designation** of the department of state as agent for service of process; 송달
▸ the **address of the office** and the name and address of the agent for service of process;
▸ the **name** and business address of each **general partner**;
▸ the **latest date** upon which the limited partnership is to **dissolve**; and
▸ any other matters the general partners determine to include therein. 결정하다

1. Name

The partnership name must contain the words **"limited partnership"** or the abbreviation **"L.P.,"** and may not contain the name of a limited partner unless it is also the name of a general partner, the corporate name of a corporate general partner, or the business of the limited partnership had been carried on under that name before the admission of that limited partner. 약자, 약어 / 허가

2. Contribution

The contribution of a limited partner may be in cash, property, or services rendered, or a promissory note or other obligation to contribute cash or property or to perform services. 채무약속 / 소유권 / 용역을 제공하다

Unless the partnership agreement provides otherwise, a partner is obligated to make the promised contribution, even if he is unable to perform because of death, disability, or any other reason. If a partner does not make the required contribution of property or services, he is obligated, at the option of the limited partnership, to contribute cash equal to that portion of the value, as stated in the partnership records, of the stated contribution that has not been made. 신체장애 / (유사개념) 상업등기

IV. Liability of Limited Partners

As a general rule, a limited partner is not liable for the

obligations of a limited partnership for any amount beyond his contribution. 금액

1. Exceptions of the Limitation

There are several exceptions to the general rule.

a) Limited Partner Participates in Control of Business

A **limited partner** who participates in control of the business is **liable as a general partner to creditors.** However, he is liable only to persons who transact business with the limited partnership reasonably believing, based upon the limited partner's conduct, that the limited partner is a general partner.

Frigidaire Sales Corporation v. Union Properties, Inc. – 562 P.2d 244 (1977)

The plaintiff Frigidaire entered into a contract with Commercial Investors, a limited partnership. Mannon and Baxter were limited partners of Commercial and also officers, directors, and shareholder of the defendant Union Properties, the only general partner of Commercial. Mannon and Baxter controlled Commercial by exercising day-to-day control and management of the defendant. Commercial breached the contract and the plaintiff filed suit against the defendant, Mannon, and Baxter, asserting that they should incur general liability for the limited partnership's obligations because thy exercised day-to-day control and management of Commercial. Mannon and Baxter argued that Commercial was controlled by the defendant, a separate legal entity, and not by them in their individual capacities. The trial court declined to hold Mannon and Baxter generally liable, and Frigidaire appealed.

(유사개념) 지배인
이사 / 주주
제소하다
주장하다
항소하다

Issue

Do limited partners incur general liability for the limited partnership's obligations simply because they are officers, directors, or shareholders of the corporate general partner?

Holding and Reasoning

No. Parties may form a limited partnership with a corporation as the sole general partner. To hold that Mannon and Baxter incurred general liability for the limited partnership's obligations would require the court to totally ignore the corporate entity of the defendant, when the plaintiff knew it was dealing with that corporate entity. Although Mannon and Baxter controlled Commercial through their control of the defendant, they scrupulously separated their actions on behalf of Commercial from their personal actions and the corporations were clearly separate entities. The plaintiff knew that Union was the sole general partner of Commercial and that Mannon and Baxter were only limited partners. If the plaintiff had not wished to rely on the solvency of the defendant as the only general partner, it could have insisted that Mannon and Baxter personally guarantee contractual performance. When the shareholders of a corporation, who are also the corporation's officers and directors, conscientiously keep the affairs of the corporation separate from their personal affairs, and no fraud or manifest injustice is perpetrated upon third persons who deal with the corporation, the corporation's separate identity should be respected.

요구하다
지불능력
강하게 주장하다
사기, 기망

b) Limited Partner's Name Used in Partnership Name

A limited partner who knowingly permits his name to be improperly included in the partnership name is liable as a general partner to creditors who are without actual knowledge that he is not a general partner.

실제 지식, 인식

2. Liability Because of the Agreement

Subject to provisions in the partnership agreement, a partner is liable for all contributions promised in the partnership agreement. Such liability may be compromised only by the consent of all of the partners.

기여

V. Rights of Limited Partners

A limited partner has the following rights:

1. Voting Right

The **partnership agreement may grant to** all or a specified group of limited partners the **right to vote** (on a per capita or other basis) upon any matter. 부여하다, 주다

2. Sharing of Profits and Losses

The **profits and losses** of a limited partnership are allocated among the partners, and among classes of partners, in the **manner provided in the partnership agreement.** If the partnership agreement does not so provide in writing, profits and losses are allocated on the basis of the value, as stated in the partnership records, of the contributions made by each partner to the extent they have been received by the partnership and have not been returned. 배분하다, 할당하다

3. Right to Information

RULPA provides each limited partner with the following rights:

- The right to inspect and copy any of the partnership books required by RULPA to be maintained; and 조사권
- The right to obtain from the general partners from time to time, upon reasonable demand, true and full information regarding the state of the business and financial condition of the limited partnership, the limited partnership's federal, state, and local income tax return, and any other information as is just and reasonable. 상태

4. Interest Assignable

Unless the partnership agreement provides otherwise, a **partnership interest is assignable in whole or in part.** An assignment of a partnership interest does not dissolve a limited partnership or entitle the assignee to become or to exercise any rights of a partner. An assignment entitles the assignee to receive, to the extent assigned, only the distribution to which the assignor would be entitled. A

양도가능한
양도
양수인(反, assigner)

partner ceases to be a partner upon assignment of all his partnership interest, unless the partnership agreement provides otherwise.

5. Business Transactions with the Partnership

Except as provided in the partnership agreement, a partner may lend money to and transact other business with the limited partnership and, subject to other applicable law, has the same rights and obligations with respect thereto as a person who is not a partner.

준거법, 적용 가능한 법

6. Withdrawal of Limited Partner

A limited partner may withdraw from a limited partnership at the time or upon the happening of events specified in the partnership agreement. If the agreement does not specify in writing the time or the events upon the happening of which a limited partner may withdraw or a definite time for the dissolution or winding up of the limited partnership, a limited partner may withdraw upon not less than six months' prior written notice to each general partner at the address on the books of the limited partnership at its office in New York.

탈퇴하다, 퇴사하다

7. Right to Dissolve

On application by or for a partner, a supreme court in the judicial district in which the office of the limited partnership is located may **decree dissolution of a limited partnership** whenever it is not reasonably practicable to carry on the business in conformity with the partnership agreement.

VI. Rights and Liabilities of a General Partner

Except as otherwise provided in RULPA or in the partnership agreement, a general partner of a limited partnership has the rights and powers and is subject to the restrictions and liabilities of a partner in a partnership without limited partners.

(대리) 권리, 권능
제한

VII. Dissolution

1. General Principles

A limited partnership is dissolved and its affairs must be wound up upon the happening of the first to occur of the following:

- At the time specified in the certificate of limited partnership;
- Upon the happening of events specified in writing in the partnership agreement;
- Upon written consent of all general partners and two-thirds of each class of limited partners;
- Upon withdrawal of a general partner; or
- Upon entry of a decree of judicial dissolution.

2. Distribution of Assets

Upon the winding up of a limited partnership, **the assets are distributed as follows:** 재산

- To creditors, including partners who are creditors, in satisfaction of liabilities of the limited partnership, other than liabilities for distributions to partners upon withdrawal;
- Except as provided in the partnership agreement, to partners and former partners in satisfaction of liabilities for distributions to partners upon withdrawal; and
- Except as provided in the partnership agreement, to partners first for the return of their contributions, and second, respecting their partnership interests, in the proportions in which the partners share in distributions.

Part 4: Law of Corporations

A. General principles

I. Characterisation

Traditionally, corporations have been characterized by six attributes. They are **limited liability, free transferability** of ownership interests, **continuity of existence, centralized management, entity status,** and **taxation of enterprise income at the entity** (corporate) level rather than directly to the shareholders (owners). In detail these attributes mean the following:

양도성

기업

1. Free Transferability of Ownership Interests

A transferee of a general partnership interest normally cannot be substituted as a partner without the unanimous consent of the remaining partners. In contrast, ownership (or also called "equity") interests in corporations represented by shares of stock are freely transferable.

양수인

만장일치로

지분에 대한 지분

2. Limited Liability

General partners are personally liable for obligations that arise out of the conduct of their business. In contrast, **shareholders of a corporation are not personally liable for corporate obligations.** This legal rule is conventionally expressed by the statement that shareholders have limited liability. Furthermore, the managers of a corporation are also normally not personally liable for corporate obligations.

제한된

회사채무

3. Continuity of Existence

Unlike partnerships, which are typically for a limited term, the **legal existence of a corporation is perpetual,** unless a shorter term is stated in the certificate of incorporation.

무제한의, 영속하는

4. Centralized Management

According to partnership law, all partners have a right to

participate in <u>management</u>. In contrast, under the corporate statutes a corporation is normally managed by or under the direction of a <u>board of directors</u>, and **a <u>shareholder</u>, as such, has no right to participate in management.**

경영

이사회 / 주주

5. Entity Status

Corporations have the status of "legal persons," or entities, while partnerships do not. At least traditionally this is so, because the status of partnerships has changed under the new laws of RUPA.

6. Taxation

A corporation is normally **<u>taxed</u> as an entity**, that is, a corporation's income is taxed to the corporation, rather than to the shareholders. If the corporation's after tax income is later distributed as a <u>dividend</u>, the dividend is taxed to the shareholders as part of their income. This effect is sometimes referred to as "double taxation".

과세하다

이익배당금

<u>II. Distinction Among Corporations</u>

There are two basic types of corporations which can be distinguished on a broad perspective. On one side there are **<u>closely held corporations</u>** and on the other side **<u>publicly held corporations</u>**. The first type of a corporation corresponds to the German GmbH and is held by a small number of shareholders where shareholders are the same persons as the managers. This form is often used by family-owned businesses. The latter type of corporation corresponds to the German AG and consists of a great number of shareholders.

(유사개념) 유한회사 / (유사개념) 주식회사

<u>III. Applicable Law</u>

The law applicable to a corporation depends on the **State law** where the corporation is located. There are no <u>federal corporate laws</u> or standardized regulations which are the single basis for State laws, although there exists a Model Business Corporate Act ("MBCA"). For several reasons the State of Delaware attracts many publicly held corporations to

연방회사법

incorporate there. About 40% of corporations listed on the New York Stock Exchange are incorporated in Delaware. 설립하다, 등록하다

Therefore in this chapter the main principles of corporate law will be described. In certain situations, we will explicitly refer to the MBCA or a specific state law, which in most cases will be a statute of either Delaware or New York law. 법률

Diagram 20

Corporations — General Principles —
• Free Transferability • Limited Liability • Continuity Existence • Centralized Management

B. Organization

I. Purpose

Ordinarily, a corporation may be organized **for any lawful business or purpose**. While some states permit a corporation to operate two or more independent lines of business, it is the general rule that a single corporation may not be formed for two or more distinct and unallied purposes. But it may be formed for two or more related purposes, and it may be active in a number of allied endeavors which may reasonably come within the intention of the purpose specified in its document of creation.

허락하다 / 관련성이 없는, 무관한 / 노력 / 의도

II. Document of Incorporation

The first step of the organization process of a corporation is to file a **"certificate of incorporation"** or the **"articles of incorporation"** or a "charter" with the relevant state official, which is usually the secretary of state. The terminology varies from state to state.

기본정관, 회사설립정관 / (州의) 내무부 장관

In Delaware it is called a "certificate of incorporation" (Delaware General Corporate Law §103(C)(1)-(3)), which has to be filed with the secretary of state.

1. Content of Filing Document

Usually, state statutes require the following minimum content, and the document that must be filed has to cover:

- ▸ the **name** of the corporation
- ▸ **duration** 기간
- ▸ its **purpose**
- ▸ the **securities** it is authorized to issue 담보
- ▸ the **name of its registered agent** and the address of its registered office
- ▸ the names and addresses of its **initial board of directors** 최초의
- ▸ the **name** and address of the **incorporator** or incorporators 설립자

2. Amendment of the Initial Document

The initial document can be amended at any time after filing. However, any class of stockholders who would be adversely affected by the amendment must approve the amendment by majority vote. 승인하다

III. Bylaws

After formation the corporation adopts bylaws. The corporation's bylaws are **rules governing the corporation's internal affairs**. This can be, for example, date, time and place for annual meeting; number of directors; listing of officers; what constitutes quorum for directors' meetings, etc. Bylaws are usually not filed with the Secretary of State, and may usually be amended by either the board or the shareholders. 정관, 자치규범 연례 사원총회

The internal affairs and management of a corporation are governed by its bylaws, which, in effect, constitute the rules and regulations enacted by the corporation for its own government. 제정하다

Regularly, corporate bylaws are **binding on stockholders**, officers and directors, all of whom, as a general rule of law, are conclusively presumed to have knowledge of all the rules governing the management of their corporation.

A corporation, by its members or stockholders, may enact any bylaws deemed necessary for the proper management of its affairs, provided that these rules are not in violation of law, public policy, or the provisions of the corporate charter itself. 간주하다

Any bylaw which is inconsistent with the charter of the corporation is ultra vires – which means it is beyond corporate powers--and therefore void. 권능을 초과하는, 월권의 무효의

Corporate bylaws may properly set forth, among other things:

- the number and duties of corporate officers;
- the method of their selection or election;
- their salaries, if any; 월급
- the number and qualifications of directors;
- the annual or other fixed corporate meeting dates;
- voting privileges and regulations; and
- the penalties for the violation of corporate rules and regulations. 벌과금

Although bylaws, generally, are presumptively valid, in specific instances, they have been held to be invalid for the following reasons (in addition to those cases where they were found to be contrary to law, public policy, or the corporate charter):

- the absolute restriction on the right of the members to sue in court 제소하다
- their unequal operation upon all persons of the particular class which they were intended to govern
- the impairment of contract rights 침해
- the imposition of personal liability on the corporate members or their release therefrom
- the disturbance of vested voting rights 확립된, 보장된
- the restraint of trade 자유거래의 제한
- violation of antitrust laws 반독점법
- unreasonable, oppressive or extortionate operation 폭리의, 착취하는, 터무니 없는

Diagram 21

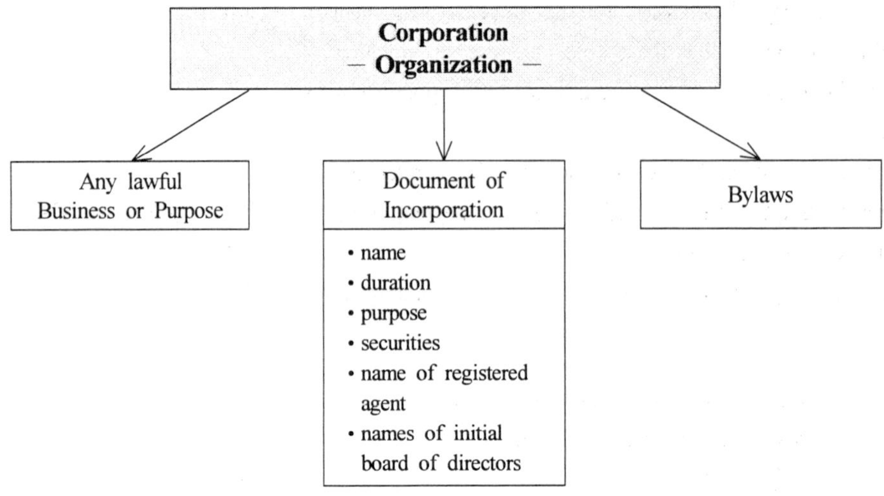

C. Transactions by Promoters Before Incorporation

A promoter is a person who, by himself or in association with others, **undertakes to form a corporation.** 발기인*

I. Basic Function of Promoters

Generally, it is a promoter's function to procure for the future corporation its articles of incorporation and the necessary financing to carry out the business purposes for which it is to be formed. Ordinarily, promoters are not agents (in the legal sense) of the prospective corporate entity. 마련하다, 조달하다 / 사업목적

In the absence of a subsequent adoption, ratification or acceptance of a contract made by the promoters, therefore, it is not binding on the corporation, nor can the corporation itself enforce it. 강제, 관철하다

II. Promoter's Liability

A promoter may occasionally be liable for debts he contracts on behalf of the corporation to-be.

The following situations may be distinguished:

1. Awareness of the Promoter

---

* 반드시 설립자 incorporator와 일치하는 것은 아님.

If the promoter enters into a contract in the corporation's name, and the promoter knows that the corporation has not yet been formed and the other party does not know this, the promoter will be liable under the contract.

But if the corporation is later formed and **"adopts"** the contract, then the **promoter may escape liability**. 책임(채무)을 벗어나다

2. Contract says that a Corporation is not Formed

If the contract entered into by the promoter on behalf of the corporation recites that the corporation has not yet been formed, the liability of the promoter depends on what the court finds to be the parties' intent. 언급하다

a) Never Formed, or Immediately Defaults

If the corporation is never formed, or it is formed but then immediately defaults, the promoter most likely will be held liable. 채무를 이행하지 않다

b) Formed and Then Adopted

If the corporation is formed, and then shows its intent to take over the contract, e.g. by adopting it, the court may find that both parties intended that the promoter be released from liability. 면제하다, 풀어주다

III. Liability of Corporation

If the corporation did not exist at the time the promoter signed a contract on its behalf, the **corporation will not become liable unless it adopts the contract.** Adoption may be implied. 채용

IV. Promoter's Fiduciary Obligations

During the pre-incorporation period, the promoter has a fiduciary obligation to the to-be-formed corporation. He therefore may not pursue his own profit at the corporation's ultimate expense. Co-promoters of a venture owe fiduciary duties to each other, to the corporation, and to subsequent final interests in the venture. 신탁의무 기업

- After the corporation is formed it may obtain from the promoter any benefits or rights the promoter obtained on its behalf.
- Any benefits or rights one promoter obtained must be shared with the co-promoters much as though they were partners.
- A major issue relating to promoters' fiduciary duties is the extent to which subsequent shareholders or investors are protected by fiduciary duties.
- Some cases have applied fiduciary concepts to protect creditors against unfair or fraudulent transactions by promoters.

D. Defective Incorporation

I. Common law "de facto" Doctrine

Under common law there was the rule that, if a person made a colorable attempt to incorporate (e.g., he submitted articles to the Secretary of State, which were rejected), a **"de facto" corporation** was found to have been formed. This would be enough to shelter the would-be incorporator from the personal liability that would otherwise result. This is the "de facto corporation" doctrine.

거절, 거부하다 / 사실상 (反, de jure)
보호하다 / 장래의, 지망하는

Nowadays, however, most states have abolished the de facto doctrine, and expressly impose personal liability on anyone who purports to do business as a corporation while knowing that incorporation has not occurred.

폐지하다, 폐기하다

II. Corporation by Estoppel

The common law also applies the "corporation by estoppel" doctrine, whereby a creditor who deals with the business as a corporation, and who agrees to look to the "corporation's" assets rather than the "shareholders'" assets will be estopped from denying the corporation's existence.

(금반언에 의한) 사실상 회사
채권자
재산

E. Piercing the Corporate Veil

The phrase "piercing the corporate veil" is a **metaphor to describe the cases in which a court refuses to recognize the separate existence of a corporation despite its proper formation.**

(기업의 베일을 뚫다, 회사의 장막을 관통하다) 회사 법인격 부인론

I. Traditional Test

The traditional tests for piercing the corporate veil are to prevent fraud and to achieve equity. Courts have also applied concepts of instrumentality or alter ego as the basis for piercing the corporate veil. Courts state that the general rule is that each corporation is independent of its shareholders and that piercing the corporate veil liability should be imposed only in extreme circumstances.

사기, 기망을 예방하다

특수한 상황

II. Individual shareholders

In a case, where the corporation's shares are held by individuals, courts emphasize some factors which are important to decide whether to pierce the corporate veil:

1. Tort vs. contract ("voluntary creditor")

Courts are more likely to pierce the veil in a tort case (where the creditor is "involuntary") than in a contract case (where the creditor is "voluntary").

2. Fraud

Veil piercing is more likely where there has been a **grievous fraud or wrongdoing** by the shareholders (e.g., the sole shareholder siphons out all profits, leaving the corporation without enough money to pay its claims).

심각한, 극악한 / 범죄, 비행

(사이펀=수관으로) 빨아내다, 소모하다

Perpetual Real Estate Services, Inc. v. Michaelson Properties — 974 F.2d 545 (1992)

The plaintiff, Perpetual Real Estate Services, Inc. and the defendant Michaelson Properties, Inc. entered into two joint venture real estate partnerships. Each corporate partner contributed to a working capital fund. The plaintiff negotiated

토지조합(=인적 결합회사)

personal guarantees from the defendant in a number of contexts. More than a year after distribution of the profits on the second partnership, some of the condominium purchasers filed suit for breach of warranty. The plaintiff paid the full amount of the settlement, then filed suit against Michaelson and the defendant, seeking indemnity and asserting that defendant's corporate veil should be pierced. The jury returned a verdict in favor of the plaintiff on the veil-piercing count. The court rejected Michaelson's motion for judgment notwithstanding the verdict. Michaelson appealed.

분양아파트
보증의무의 위반
화해
면책
기각하다

Issue

Where a sole shareholder exercises undue domination and control over the corporation, will the corporate veil be pierced only if the sole shareholder also used the corporate form to obscure fraud or conceal crime?

과도한 / 지배(력)

Holding and Reasoning

Yes. Even if the defendant were Michaelson's alter ego, there is no evidence that Michaelson used the corporation to obscure fraud or conceal crime. Parties to a commercial transaction must be free to negotiate questions of limited liability and to enforce their agreements by recourse to the law of contracts. The second joint venture included no personal guarantees by Michaelson. As a matter of contract, then, Michaelson was entitled to insulation from personal liability on the claims, and it is not the court's place to restructure the parties' agreement.

숨기다, 은폐하다
보호, 격리

3. Inadequate Capitalization

Most important, veil piercing is most likely if the corporation has been inadequately capitalized. But most **courts do not make inadequate capitalization alone enough for veil piercing.**

a) Zero Capital

When the shareholder invests no money whatsoever in the corporation, courts are especially likely to pierce the veil, and may require less of a showing on the other factors than if the capitalization was inadequate but non-zero.

Sea-Land Services, Inc. v. Pepper Source – 941 F.2d 519 (7th Cir. 1991)

After the plaintiff Sea-Land, an ocean carrier, shipped peppers for the defendant Pepper Source, it could not collect on the substantial freight bill because the defendant had been dissolved. Moreover, the defendant apparently had no assets. Unable to recover on a default judgment against defendant, the plaintiff filed another law suit, seeking to pierce the corporate veil and hold Marchese, sole shareholder of the defendant and other corporations, personally liable. The defendant then took the necessary steps to be reinstated as a corporation in Illinois. The plaintiff moved for summary judgment, which the court granted. Marchese and the defendant appealed.

공급하다

궐석판결

1인 주주

원상회복하다, 재설립하다

Issue

Will the corporate veil be pierced where there is a unity of interest and ownership between a corporation and an individual and where adherence to the fiction of a separate corporate existence would sanction a fraud or promote injustice?

고수, 집착

Holding and Reasoning

Yes. The corporate veil will be pierced where there is a unity of interest and ownership between a corporation and an individual and where adherence to the fiction of a separate corporate existence would sanction a fraud or promote injustice.

There can be no doubt that the unity of interest and ownership part of the test is met here. Corporate records and formalities have not been maintained, funds and assets have been commingled with abandon, defendant was undercapitalized, and corporate assets have been moved and tapped and borrowed without regard to their source. The second part of the test is more problematic, however. An unsatisfied judg-

혼합하다 / 포기하다

ment, by itself, is not enough to show that injustice would be promoted. On remand, the plaintiff is required to show the kind of injustice necessary to invoke the court's power to prevent injustice.

b) Siphoning

Capitalization may be inadequate either because there is not enough initial capital, or because the corporation's profits are **systematically siphoned out as earned**. But if capitalization is adequate, and the corporation then has unexpected liabilities, the shareholders' failure to put in additional capital will generally not be inadequate capitalization.

빼돌리다, 밖으로 빨아내다

4. Failure of Formalities

Lastly, the court is more likely to pierce the veil if the shareholders have failed to follow corporate formalities in running the business.

III. Parent/Subsidiary

If shares are held by a parent corporation, the court may pierce the veil and make the parent corporation liable for the debts of the subsidiary.

1. No Liability Generally

Again, the general rule is that the corporate parent shareholder is not liable for the debts of the subsidiary (just as individual shareholders are not liable for the corporation's debts).

2. Factors

But as in the individual-shareholder case, certain acts by the parent may cause veil piercing to take place. Such factors include:

- failure to follow separate corporate formalities for the two corporations (e.g., both have the same board, and do not hold separate directors' meetings);

- ▸ the subsidiary and parent are operating pieces of the same business, and the **subsidiary is <u>undercapitalized</u>;** (기업에) 충분한 자본을 공급하지 않다
- ▸ the **public is misled** about which entity is operating which business;
- ▸ **assets are intermingled** as between parent and subsidiary; or
- ▸ the subsidiary is operated in an unfair manner (e.g., forced to sell at cost to parent).

<u>IV. Brother/Sister ("Enterprise Liability")</u>

Occasionally, the court may treat brother/sister corporations (i.e., those having a common parent) as really being one individual enterprise, in which case each will be liable for the debts of its "<u>siblings</u>." This is the "enterprise liability" theory. 형제자매

<u>F. Corporate Finance</u>

<u>I. Introduction</u>

Generally, there are four sources of capital for a corporation:

- ▸ **<u>Equity capital</u>**: Capital contributed by investors in exchange for shares of stock is called "equity capital". 자기자본
- ▸ **<u>Loans</u> from shareholders**: Capital loaned by the shareholders to the corporation may be substituted for equity capital in whole or in part. 대출
- ▸ **Loans from third persons**: Capital loaned by third persons to the corporation is usually referred to as "debt financing" and should be distinguished from loans by shareholders because of the significantly different economic and legal consequences of such loans.
- ▸ **Capital internally generated from the corporation's business** through the <u>retention</u> of earnings, creation of <u>reserves</u>, sales of appreciated assets and the like is a final source of funds needed by a corporation. 보류, 유지 / 예비금, 준비금

<u>II. The Issuance of Common Shares</u>

The articles of incorporation must set forth the number of shares the corporation is authorized to issue. If the corporation is authorized to issue more than one class of shares, the number of shares of each class, and a distinguishing designation for each class, must also be set forth.

1. Common Shares

It is not necessary to describe the rights of common shares in the articles of incorporation. The two basic rights of common shares are:

- **entitlement to vote**, and
- **entitlement of the net assets** of the corporation when distributions are made or upon dissolution

2. Par Value

The articles of incorporation must, however, state the par value of the shares of each class. Some states have eliminated the concept of par value. The current trend is towards the elimination of this concept in additional states. (증권 등의) 액면가격

Par value is an arbitrary value associated with shares of stock. The par value of shares set forth in the articles of incorporation and appears on the face of certificates for shares.

3. Price of Shares

There is no minimum issue price for shares. The price at which shares are issued is set by the board of directors, and so long as all shares being issued at the same time are issued at the same price, any price may be set by the board.

In states with par value statutes, the board of directors may set the price at which shares are issued, but **shares should never be issued for less than par value.**

But if, nevertheless, par value shares are issued under par value, the consequence is the creation of "watered shares" and this results in a liability on the part of the recipient to pay to the corporation the difference between par value and

희석한 주식

수령인

what the shareholder actually paid.

III. Issuance of More Than a Single Class of Shares

Common shares are the residual ownership interests in the corporation. Other classes of shares with limited or preferred rights may also be created. The terms "common shares" and "preferred shares" are widely used in practice.

남은, 잔여의

1. Preferred Shares

Preferred means that shares have preference over common shares either as to dividends or on liquidation or both. A preference simply means that the preferred shares are entitled to a payment of a specified amount before the common shares are entitled to anything. Most preferred shares have **both dividend and liquidation preferences.**

이익배당금

2. Equivalence of Shares Within a Class or Series

All shares of a class or series must have identical preference, limitations and relative rights with those of other shares of the same series or class. This requirement is a matter of controversy in some defensive tactics against take-overs where the corporation may distinguish between holders of the same class of shares on the basis of outside event.

Diagram 22

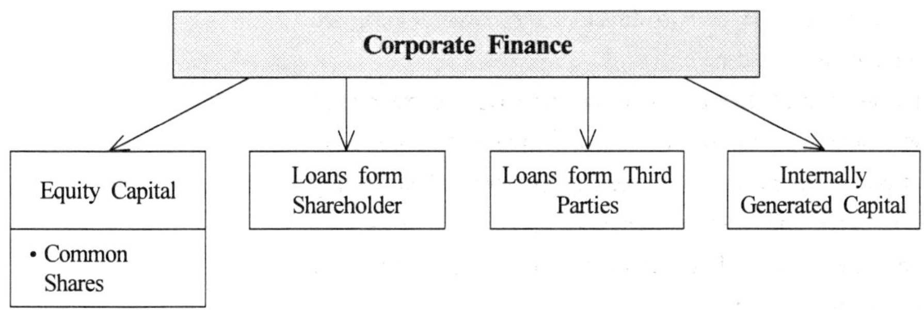

G. Statutory Scheme of Management and Control

Generally, three groups manage and control the corporation:

- **Shareholder**: Shareholders are the ultimate owners of the corporation. Because of the separation of ownership and control, they have only limited power of management and control. Their power is exercised indirectly through the election or removal of directors. 선출 / 해임, 면직
- **Directors**: Directors have general powers of management and control. In large, publicly held corporations, they oversee the management rather than actually managing.
- **Officers**: In theory, they carry out directors' decisions rather than make policy decisions though officers may be delegated decision-making authority and have some inherent power.
    - In publicly held corporations, officers in fact exercise virtually complete control over day-to-day matters.
    - In closely held corporations, the shareholders and directors are also usually the principal officers of the corporation.

H. Directors

1. Number and Changes

Today, most states permit a board of directors to consist of one or more directors. Historically, three directors were required and a few states retain this requirement. Some states allow boards of one or two directors only where there are one or two shareholders. 보유하다, 존속시키다

The **number of directors may be increased or decreased** by amendments to the bylaws, but a decrease does not have the effect of eliminating or shortening the term of any sitting director. Since the directors generally have power to amend bylaws, the board of directors in effect has power to determine its own size.

Some cases recognize that bylaws setting the number of directors may be amended informally, e.g. by electing four directors when the bylaws provide for only three directors. This is not a desirable practice since it injects future uncertainty as to the number of directors to be elected and reduces the value of the written bylaws. (문서로 작성된) 정관, 자치 규약

II. Meetings, Quorums and Notice

Regular meetings of the board occur at the times specified in the bylaws. Special meetings may be called by the persons specified in the bylaws.

1. Notice

Unlike shareholders' meetings, **directors' meetings may occur without notice** or with only such notice as provided by the bylaws. Special meetings may require notice of two days or more. A director waives objection to defects in a notice of meeting if he participates in the meeting.

2. Quorum

A quorum consists of a majority of the board of directors unless a higher percentage is required by the bylaws. An exception is made to fill vacancies on the board. The MBCA of 1984 also permits the quorum requirement to be reduced to one-third of the directors. 공석, 결원

3. Voting

Directors vote on a per capita basis. A majority vote of those present at a meeting where a quorum is present is necessary for the board to act. The bylaws may increase the vote necessary for approval of an action up to and including unanimity.

III. Compensation

Directors traditionally **serve without compensation.** But, publicly held corporations usually provide substantial compensation for outside directors. Compensation increasingly is in the form of shares of the corporation. 봉급

IV. Resignation and Removal

The MBCA of 1984 permits resignation either immediately or at a future date. Most state statutes do not expressly cover the resignation of directors. In the case of a resignation at a future date, the resigning director may participate in decisions before that date, including the selection of his successor.

In most states directors may be removed by shareholders, with or without cause. Articles of incorporation, however, may limit the power of removal to removal for cause. Removal by judicial action is also authorized under the statutes of some states.

V. Filling of Vacancies

If a vacancy occurs, it may be **filled either by the board of directors or the shareholders.** A few states distinguish between filling vacancies (which may be done by the board of directors) and filling newly created directorships (which may be done only by the shareholders).

Directors hold office until their successors are qualified. As a result, directors in office upon a deadlock of shareholders remain in office indefinitely.

successors: 후계자, 승계인
deadlock: 고착상태

VI. Decisions

The common law permits directors to act only at meetings, apparently to protect minority shareholders and ensure the benefit of mutual interchange and discussion. Directors may **not vote by proxy** or by seriatim approval (one after another). The rigidity of this rule has been relaxed by statute in certain areas: action by informal written consent, telephonic meetings, and by application of principles of estoppel and waiver. But the rule retains some force.

minority shareholders: 소수주주
proxy: 위임장, 대리투표
waiver: 포기

VII. Duties of Care and Loyalty

Directors owe a duty of loyalty to the corporation that prohibits self-dealing and usurpation of corporate opportunities. Directors also owe a duty of care to the corporation, though many actions may be protected by the business

duty of loyalty: 신의의무
usurpation: 불법적 권리침해, 탈취
duty of care: 주의의무

judgment rule.

1. Insider Trading

As a general rule, any shareholder may acquire or dispose of his shares as his self-interest dictates. However, where the shareholder is also a director or officer (or, by analogy, a controlling shareholder), certain rules imposing special standards of conduct come into play, depending on the circumstances.

a) Dealing with Noninsider Shareholders

Directors are held somewhat as fiduciaries to other shareholders with whom they deal in the corporation's shares. 수탁자

b) Dealing with Corporation

Directors have a fiduciary duty to the corporation, and this extends to **sales by directors of the corporation's shares to the corporation.** However, the mere fact that the price received from the corporation exceeds current market price does not, in itself, constitute a breach of this fiduciary duty, absent other proof of unfairness or undue advantage. 증거 / 과도한

c) Exploiting Inside Information in Market Trading

If directors or officers profit from market trading in the corporation's securities through use of **"inside" information gained in their official positions,** they must account for the profits to the corporation. 결산하다, 회계 보고하다

Securities and Exchange Commission (SEC) v. Texas Gulf Sulphur Co. – 401 F.2d 883 (1968)

The defendant discovered a potentially promising ore site. 철광석 탄광
Defendant's employees were ordered to keep information 근로자
regarding the site secret so that the defendant could continue testing and could purchase surrounding land at a price beneficial to the defendant. While not disclosing the 공개하다
information to the public, numerous of defendant's employees bought defendant stock and call options, anticipating an

increase in the price of defendant's stock. After rumors of the strike hit the press, defendant issued a press release denying any significant discoveries. Several days later, defendant confirmed the discovery of a vast mineral strike, sending defendant's stock soaring. The plaintiff, SEC, brought an action against several of defendant's employees for insider trading and against the defendant for dissemination of a misleading press release. The trial court ruled in favor of the defendant and its employees. The SEC appealed.

발견
광장한, 거대한
급상승하다
전파, 유포, 선전

Issues

1. Is it unlawful to trade on material inside information until such information has been disclosed to the public and has had time to become equally available to all investors?

2. Is a company press release considered to have been issued in connection with the purchase or sale of a security for purposes of imposing liability under the federal securities laws and will liability flow therefrom if a reasonable investor, in the exercise of due care, would have been misled by it?

Holding and Reasoning

1. Yes. It is unlawful to trade on material inside information until such information has been disclosed to the public and has had time to become equally available to all investors. Rule 10b-5 of the SEC is based on the justifiable expectation of the securities marketplace that all investors have equal access to material information. Anyone in possession of material nonpublic information cannot properly trade on that information, even if he is forbidden by the company from disclosing it to the public, until it has been publicly disseminated. In this case, all transactions in defendant stock or calls by those employees apprised of the exploratory drilling results were made in violation of Rule 10b-5.

정당화할 수 있는
본질적인

2. Yes. A company press release is considered to have been issued in connection with the purchase or sale of a security purposes of imposing liability under the federal securities laws, and liability will flow if a reasonable investor, in the exercise of due care, would have been misled

by it. The purchase or sale requirement under §10b of the Securities Exchange Act requires merely that the deceptive device employed be likely to cause a reasonable investor, exercising due care, to have been misled. Defendant's press release could satisfy this test, although the lower court did not properly apply this standard to the facts before it.

현혹시키는

2. Sale of Office

An officer or director must account to the corporation for amounts received as payment for turning over his corporate office to another. However, where directors sell their controlling shares for a price exceeding "fair value," the mere existence of the differential does not mean there was an unlawful sale of office.

3. Business Judgment Rule

The **Business Judgement Rule** was developed in the famous case of Auerbach v. Bennett.

Auerbach v. Bennett – 393 N.E.2d 994 (1979)

With the assistance of special counsel and Arthur Anderson & Co., the defendant GTE's audit committee conducted an investigation into GTE's world-wide operations. The audit committee subsequently released its report, which stated that evidence had been found that, in the period from 1971 to 1975, GTE had made payments abroad and in the United States constituting bribes and kickbacks totaling more than $ 11,000,000, and that some directors had been involved. The plaintiff Auerbach, a shareholder, instituted a derivative action on behalf of GTE against GTE's directors, Arthur Anderson, and GTE, alleging breach of corporate duties and seeking damages as reimbursement for the wrongful payments. The board of directors then adopted a resolution creating a special litigation committee to investigate the derivative action and determine which position GTE should take. The committee

뇌물

파생소송*
(=주주 대표소송 representative action)
변상(배상)하다

* 이사진에 대한 손해배상 청구권은 1차적으로 회사에 속한 것이며, 주주 개인의 소송은 회사소유의 1차적 청구권에서 "파생"한 것이다.

comprised three disinterested directors who had joined the board after the alleged transaction had occurred. The committee concluded that Arthur Anderson had acted in accordance with generally accepted auditing standards and in good faith and that no proper interest of GTE or its shareholders would be served by continuing the claim against it. The committee also found that the claims against the individual directors were without merit. GTE's general counsel filed for and was granted summary judgment. Another shareholder was substituted as plaintiff and appealed.

포함하다

Issue

May a court inquire as to the adequacy and appropriateness of a special litigation committee's investigative procedures and methodologies?

상당성

Holding and Reasoning

Yes. A court may properly inquire as to the adequacy and appropriateness of a special litigation committee's investigative procedures and methodologies, but may not consider factors under the domain of business judgment. The business judgment doctrine recognizes that courts are ill-equipped to evaluate what are and essentially must be business judgments. However, the rule shields the deliberations and conclusions of a special committee only if its members possess disinterested independence and do not stand in a dual relation that would prevent an unprejudicial exercise of judgment. In this case there is nothing in the record to raise a triable issue of fact as to the independence and disinterested status of the three directors on the special litigation committee, or as to the sufficiency and appropriateness of the investigative procedures they employed. The derivative suit was brought against only four members of the fifteen-member board, and the three members of the special litigation committee joined the board after the alleged transactions occurred. To disqualify an entire board would be to render a corporation powerless to make an effective business judgment with respect to prosecution of a derivative action. The decision of the disinterested special litigation committee forecloses further judicial inquiry.

보호하다 / 심의, 토의

배제하다, 제외하다

VIII. Liabilities and Suits Against Directors and Officers

There are certain other duties imposed on directors which go beyond those described above.

1. Statutory Liabilities of Directors

Some states impose on directors certain liabilities by statute.

Directors may be **jointly and severally liable** to the corporation (or its creditors and shareholders) if they "vote for or concur in" any of the following: 공동으로 책임지는

- ▶ The declaration of a dividend or other distribution contrary to the BCL or certificate of incorporation;
- ▶ A repurchase by the corporation of its own shares contrary to the BCL or certificate of incorporation;
- ▶ A distribution of assets after dissolution without adequately providing for known liabilities of the corporation; or
- ▶ The making of any loan to a director without the required shareholder approval.

Liability is limited to the extent of injury as a result of prohibited actions.

Directors are jointly and severally liable, but any director against whom a claim is asserted is entitled to contribution from the other directors who are liable. Furthermore,

shareholders who knowingly received improper distributions or payments for shares may be liable to the directors held liable.

Francis v. United Jersey Bank – 432 A.2d 814 (1981)

Defendant Pritchard inherited a 48 % interest in Pritchard and Baird, a reinsurance broker, from her husband. She and her two sons, Charles and William, served as directors of the corporation. Her sons withdrew over $ 12 million in the form of loans from client trust accounts. Defendant was completely ignorant as to the fundamentals of the reinsurance

상속하다
재보험

business, and paid no attention to the affairs of the corporation. The trial court held her liable for the client's losses, finding that although she was competent to act, she had made no effort to exercise her duties as a director.

Issue

Does individual liability of a corporation's directors to its clients require a duty, a breach, and proximate cause? 근인, 직접원인, 인과관계

Holding and Reasoning

Yes. Individual liability of a corporation's directors to its clients requires a demonstration that a duty existed, the directors breached that duty, and the breach was proximate cause of the client's losses. This is a departure from the general rule that a director is immune from liability and is not an insurer of the corporation's success. 성공 The director of a corporation stands in a fiduciary relationship to both the corporation and its stockholders. Inherent in this role is a duty to acquire a basic understanding of the corporation's business, and a continuing duty to keep informed of its activities. This entails (~을 결과로서) 수반하다 an overall monitoring of the corporation's affairs, and a regular review of its financial statements. Such a review may represent a duty of further inquiry. Here, the defendant failed to exercise supervision over the corporation, including the examination of its financial statements, which would have revealed 폭로하다 the misappropriation of funds by her sons. The cumulative effect of her negligence was a substantial factor contributing to the clients' loss.

2. Persons who May Bring Action

An action based on **approval of unlawful dissipations** under section 719 or for **relief for misconduct** under section 720 may be brought by any of the following:

- The corporation;
- A receiver, trustee in bankruptcy, or judgment creditor of the corporation;
- An officer or director of the corporation; or

- A shareholder (of record or beneficial) or voting trust certificate holder, provided the conditions for derivative action are met.

Energy Resources Corp., Inc. v. Porter – 438 NE.2d 391 (Mass. App. Ct. 1982)

The defendant, vice president and chief scientist of the plaintiff, entered into an agreement with two of his colleagues from Howard University to pursue a development grant from the Department of Energy. Howard served as a primary applicant, and the plaintiff as the subcontractor. Defendant's colleagues were concerned that plaintiff's involvement in the proposal would negatively affect their ability to obtain the grant, so they suggested that the defendant form his own corporation and substitute it for plaintiff. Defendant formed EEE for this purpose, and Howard awarded the grant. Defendant immediately resigned from the plaintiff. Plaintiff sued defendant for breaching his duty to protect plaintiff's interests. The trial court found for defendant on the theory that the project no longer represented a corporate opportunity for plaintiff when his colleagues suggested he form an independent corporation.

과학자, 학자

하청계약자

Issue

May an officer or director of a corporation, who has seized an opportunity of that corporation for his personal benefit, invoke the refusal to deal as a defense?

붙잡다

Holding and Reasoning

Yes. If an officer or director of a corporations seeks to invoke refusal to deal as a defense to a charge that he seized a corporate opportunity, he must first disclose the refusal to the corporation along with a statement of reasons for the refusal. An officer or director of a corporation has a fiduciary duty not to usurp opportunities within the scope of the corporation's activities for his personal benefit. However, when that company is unable to take advantage of such an opportunity, as when the other party refuses to deal with the

신탁의무(수탁자의 의무)

corporation, the officer is then permitted to capitalize on it. First, though, he must disclose the refusal to the corporation, accompanied by a statement supporting its rationale. Defendant not only failed to disclose the refusal to plaintiff, but misrepresented his reasons for resigning from the plaintiff.

허락하다

부정확하게 설명하다

J. Officers

I. Statutory Designations of Corporate Officers

State corporation statutes contain only a few provisions dealing with corporate officers, their authority and roles. More detailed provisions usually appear in the bylaws or in resolutions adopted by the board of directors.

결의

1. Traditional Statutes

According to traditional statutes each corporation must have a **president**, a **treasurer**, a **secretary**, and (usually) one or more **vice presidents** and may have such additional officers with such authority as the board of directors deem appropriate. These statutes also provide that a person can fill two or more statutory offices simultaneously except the offices of president and secretary. This exception apparently was based on the belief that execution of documents required signatures of two officers, one executing the document and the other attesting to the execution.

재무이사

2. Flexible Modern Statutes

MBCA of 1984 and Delaware General Corporate Law do **not designate specific officer titles**, granting each corporation freedom to determine which officers it chooses to have and what authority each should have. These statutes recognize that little purpose is served by statutorily designated titles which may create problems of implied or apparent authority. However these statutes recognize that there must be an officer performing the functions usually associated with the office of the corporate secretary under traditional statutes.

II. Authority of Officers in General

Persons dealing with a corporate officer generally must satisfy themselves of the officer's authority.

1. Oral Representations by Officer

As it is generally true in agency law, a representation by an agent as to the scope of his agency is not binding on the principal. 대리에 관한 법

2. Reliance on Officer's Title

Since corporate officers have only limited inherent authority, reliance on an officer's title is unlikely to provide assurance that a specific act is authorized. 신뢰, 의리

3. Reliance on Certified Resolution

Obtaining a resolution of the board of directors certified by the secretary of the corporation is the traditional method of assuring that a corporation is bound by the officer's action. It makes no difference whether or not the resolution is actually authorized by the board of directors since the corporation is bound by the secretary's certificate unless the third person knows that the resolution was not adopted.

III. Duties of Officers

Also corporate officers and agents owe a duty to the corporation of honesty, good faith, and diligence. The scope of an officer's or agent's obligation to the corporation is determined in part by the nature of his employment with the corporation. 빚지다 정직 / 성실, 주의

Bayer v. Beran — 49 N.Y.S.2d 2 (1949)

Prior to 1942, Celanese Corporation of America engaged in an advertising campaign aimed at developing brand awareness. Following a Federal Trade Commission ruling that it must label its products "rayon", Celanese commenced a 브랜드 인조견(비단)

radio advertising program costing one million dollars per year. This decision was made following studies conducted by Celanese's advertising department, and the employment of both a radio consultant and an advertising agency. Mrs. Dreyfus, wife of Celanese's president, was selected to perform in the radio program. The board was charged with commencing an illegal radio advertising program, negligence in its selection of the program and their decision to renew its contract, and self-interest in initiating the program and spending large sums of money in connection with it.

Issue

May the court question decisions of business management made by a corporation's board of directors?

Holding and Reasoning

No. Policies of business management are left solely to the discretion of the board of directors and may not be questioned absent a showing of fraud, improper motive, or self-interest, even though the decision may later be judged unwise or unprofitable. However, the business judgment rule only protects directors from personal liability for their negligence if they have not violated their duty of loyalty to the corporation. In cases where directors enter into personal transactions with their companies, such transactions are rigorously scrutinized and, upon the showing of any unfair advantage, will be voided. The burden then shifts to the interested director to demonstrate the transaction's good faith and inherent fairness to the corporation. In this case, there is no evidence that the advertising program was inefficient, disproportionate in price, or conducted for the personal gain of Mrs. Dreyfus.

재량
이익이 남지 않는
검사하다
무효선언하다
증거

IV. Liability

Corporate officers are not liable on corporate obligations in which they participate as agents except in the following circumstances:

1. Express Guarantee

Under the <u>statute of frauds</u> a personal guarantee of a corporate obligation may **have to be in writing**. 형식요건

2. Confusion of Roles

An officer may not clearly <u>delineate</u> that he is acting as an agent and may therefore become personally liable under agency or estoppel principles. 묘사, 서술하다

3. Statutory Liability

A few statutes provide for officer liability for certain types of corporate obligations, e.g. the provision of the Internal Revenue Code that imposes personal liability on officers who are required to collect employee withholding taxes.

4. Personal Participation in Tortious Conduct

A corporate officer is **personally liable if he personally participates in <u>tortious</u> conduct**. 불법행위의

5. Actions in Excess of Authority

A corporate officer may be personally liable on contracts or other obligations entered into in the name of the corporation if the officer <u>exceeds</u> his actual authority to bind the corporation. The corporation is bound if the action is within the officer's apparent authority but may have an action over against the officer for exceeding his actual authority. 초과하다, 월권하다

<u>V. Tenure of Officers and Agents</u> 재직기간

Officers and agents generally serve at the will of the electing or appointing authority.

1. Employment Contracts in General

Election or appointment does not of itself create a contractual right. However, officers or agents **may be given <u>employment contracts</u>** which give rise to a claim for breach 근로계약

in the event of a premature termination of the relationship. An employment contract may extend beyond the term of the office. 너무 이른, 조기의

2. Lifetime Employment Contracts

Lifetime employment contracts are not favored. A claim that such a contract was given to an officer or employee, usually based on parole testimony, is viewed as being inherently improbable. 구두의

3. Discharge for Cause

Officers or agents with employment contracts may be discharged for cause. It is unnecessary to consider the issue of "cause" if the officer or employee does not have an employment contract. 면직, 해임하다

Diagram 23

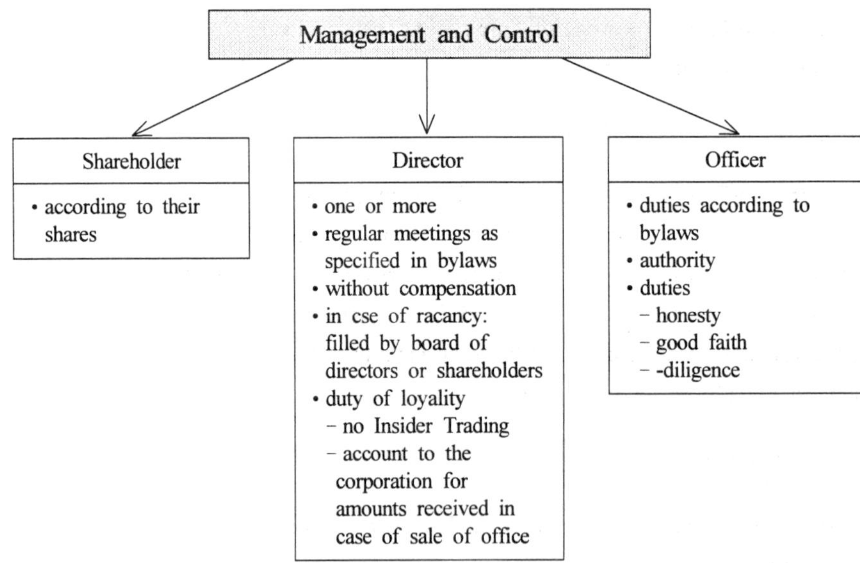

K. Shareholders' Rights and Powers

Although shareholders are the actual owners of the corporation they do not take part in the direct management of the business. Certain rules regulate that shareholders can 소유자

exercise their right to control the corporation.

I. Rights in Management of Corporation

1. No Management of Day-to-day Business

Shareholders have **no right to manage** the day-to-day business of corporate affairs. The **management** of the **corporation is located in the board of directors**. 일상적 사업

2. Certain Methods to Control

But shareholders may use certain methods of control to attain their goals. These methods are:

- **Election of directors** (by a plurality of the votes cast unless the certificate of incorporation provides for a greater proportion or for cumulative voting); 선거
- **Amendment of the certificate of incorporation** (generally requires a majority of the votes of shares entitled to vote); and 개정, 변경
- **Approval of organizational change**, such as merger, sale of assets, or dissolution. 합병

3. Special Provision for "Nonpublic" Corporations

Subject to certain conditions, "closely held" corporations may confer ordinary management powers upon shareholders. This requires a provision in the certificate of incorporation.

II. Shareholders' Meetings

The bylaws may designate reasonable procedures for the **calling and conduct of shareholders' meetings** (e.g., who may call and conduct the meeting, the means for establishing the order of business at the meeting, the procedures and requirements for nominating directors). 결정하다 소집하다

A meeting of the shareholders must be held annually, on a date fixed by or under the bylaws, for the election of directors and the transaction of other business.

Special meetings may be called by the board or by such person(s) as may be authorized by the certificate of incorporation or the bylaws.

1. Place of Meetings

Meetings of the shareholders may be held anywhere, within or outside the state, as may be fixed by or under the bylaws. Most statutes provide for the case that no place is fixed, that the meeting is to be held at the office of the corporation.

2. Notice

Written notice of the meeting must be given in a certain time before the meeting to each shareholder entitled to vote. Many state statutes provide a notice time between 10 and 60 days before the meeting.

권리있는

3. Eligibility to Vote

자격, 적격

According to most state statutes every shareholder of record is entitled to one vote for each share shown by the record to be held by the shareholder, unless otherwise provided in the certificate of incorporation (which may deny, limit, or otherwise define voting rights of any class or series).

The day as of which eligibility to vote is determined is known as the "**record date.**" Unless the bylaws provide for fixing the record date, it may be fixed in advance by the board of directors. The record date may not be less than 10 or more than 60 days before the date of the meeting. If no record date is fixed, the record date is the close of business on the day next preceding the notice date (or if no notice is given, then the day next preceding the meeting date).

이사회

앞선, 선행하는

Under certain statutorily provided circumstances, a person other than the record holder may vote shares at a shareholders' meeting.

Neither treasury shares nor shares held by a controlled corporation (i.e., a majority of whose shares entitled to vote in the election of directors is held by the corporation) may be voted or counted in determining the total number of shares outstanding.

A corporation may, in its certificate of incorporation,

confer upon the holders of any bonds the right to vote in the election of directors or on any other matters upon which shareholders may vote. 수여하다, 이전하다 / 채권

III. Proxy Rules

The so called proxy rules determine **whether or not or under which conditions a shareholder may authorize another person to act for him at the shareholders meeting.** (주주) 대리에 관한 규정

According to many state laws shareholders entitled to vote at a meeting may authorize another person to act for them by proxy.

1. Form of Proxy Authorization

Many state statutes do not specify the form required to appoint a proxy. The Business Corporate Law of New York, for example, does set forth a few nonexclusive suggestions for the form of the authorization: 제안

A shareholder may **grant a proxy in a writing** signed by the shareholder or its authorized officer, director, employee, or agent. A facsimile signature is valid. Alternatively, a shareholder may telegram, cablegram, or use other electronic means to transmit the proxy to the proxy holder, and such proxy will be valid if it is accompanied by some means for determining that it was authorized by the shareholder. 가능성, 수단

2. Expiration of Proxy Authorization

Most statutes provide that proxies are valid for only a certain time period. Regularly this period is shorter than the period between the regular shareholders meetings.

3. Revocability of Proxy

Most statutes **allow the shareholder** who executed a proxy **to revoke it later**. 취소하다, 철회하다

IV. Voting Rights

Generally, every emitted share, regardless of its class, is (외부에) 발행한

entitled to one vote. But the articles of incorporation may deny, limit, or otherwise define the voting rights of any class or series.

1. Quorum

The quorum consists of all present shareholders. It is not broken by withdrawal of shareholders. There are three kinds of quorums:

- **Normal quorum**: majority of votes of shares entitled to vote. 권리를 부여하다(hier : 권리 있는)
- **Lesser quorum**: may be provided by certificate of incorporation or bylaws (but not less than one-third).
- **Greater quorum**: may be provided only in certificate of incorporation.

2. Certain Requirements

a) Election of Directors

Directors are elected by a **plurality of votes** cast.

b) Other Action

Ordinarily, other action requires a majority of the votes cast. An abstention does not count as a vote cast. 기권(표)

c) Cumulative Voting

Absent cumulative voting, each director is elected in an independent election and a shareholder is entitled to cast only as many votes for each directorship as he has shares. For example, if a shareholder has four shares of X Corp. and there is an election for three directors, the shareholder may cast four votes for each of three candidates. In cumulative voting, each share is entitled to as many votes as there are directors being elected, and the shareholder may cast all his votes for a single candidate or divide his votes as he sees fit. For example, the shareholder described above could cast all 12 of his votes for a single candidate, or cast 10 votes for one candidate and one vote for each of two other candidates, etc. 누적적 투표

V. Class Voting

The articles of incorporation may require that certain specified classes or series of shares shall vote as a class, either generally or as to specified matters. This kind of vote is in addition to any other required vote. If any class or series of shares or bonds is entitled to elect directors as a class, removal may be effected only by the electing class.

VI. Voting Trusts

A voting trust is a written agreement of shareholders under which their shares are **transferred to a "trustee"** who votes the shares in accordance with the provisions of the agreement. The voting trustee is in this situation the legal owner of the shares. For this purpose the shares are transferred to his name as voting trustee on the corporate records. The voting trustee holds the certificates for the shares and issues "voting trust certificates" to the beneficial owners.

피신탁인, 수탁자

양도, 이전하다

Voting trustees occupy a position of trust and may be removed by the court for violating their trust or being otherwise unfit persons to remain as trustees.

Ramos v. Estrada – 8 Cal. App. 4th 1070 (1992)

Broadcast Group and Ventura 41 combined to form Television, Inc., for the purpose of establishing a Spanish language television station. Broadcast Group was owned 50% by the plaintiff and the defendant and four other couples each owned 10%. The shareholders of Broadcast Group entered an agreement to vote their shares in Television, Inc. in accordance with the majority view. In addition, the contract placed restrictions on transfer, and treated a shareholder's noncompliance with the voting provision as an election to sell his shares. Defendant voted in opposition to Broadcast Group's majority, and declared the agreement void. Plaintiff sued defendant for breach of contract. The trial court held the defendant in breach of contract, ordered their shares

다수의견

in Television, Inc., sold, and restrained them from further voting their shares in voting of the shareholder's agreement. Defendant appealed.

하지 못하게 하다, 막다

Issue

Is a shareholder agreement to vote shares in accordance with the will of the majority a valid contract?

Holding and Reasoning

Yes. Voting agreements binding individual shareholders to vote in concurrence with the majority constitute valid contracts. Although Broadcast Group did not qualify as a closely held corporation, the court upheld the contract, recognizing that voting agreements are valid in various other corporate forms. The agreement purports to limit transferability of shares consistent with the theme of effectuating the majority's interests. It expressly provides that in the event of a member's failure to vote in accordance with the majority, the member effectively elects to sell his shares to the other members. The agreement further provides for the remedy of specific performance in the event of a breach. The defendant's departure from the majority constituted a breach of the agreement, and an election to sell their interest in Television, Inc.

일치

~을 취지로 하다, 주장하다

(계약채무의) 이행

VII. Dividends

A dividend is a **cash payment made by a corporation to its common shareholders pro rata**. It is usually paid out of the current earnings of the corporation, and thus represents a partial distribution of profits.

수입

1. Generally

The decision to pay a dividend must always be made by the board of directors.

All states place certain legal limits (mostly financial ones) on the board's right to pay dividends, and directors who disregard these limits may be liable. In most states, a dividend may be paid only if both of the following general kinds of requirements are satisfied: (1) payment of the dividend will not impair the corporation's stated capital; and (2) payment will not render the corporation insolvent. 감하다, 손상하다 / 정해진 자본, 기초자본

a) Capital Tests

In most states, there are "earned surplus" restrictions: **dividends may be paid only out of the profits which the corporation has accumulated.** A substantial minority of states merely prohibit dividends that would "impair the capital" of the corporation. These states are less strict than the "earned surplus" states: they allow the payment of dividends from either earned surplus or unearned surplus. 잉여

b) Nimble Dividends

There are some states that allow payment of "nimble dividends." These are **dividends paid out of the current earnings of the corporation,** even though the corporation otherwise would not be entitled to pay the dividends (because it has no earned surplus in an earned-surplus state, or because payment would impair its stated capital in an impairment-of-capital state). 재빠른

c) Insolvency Test

Even if a dividend payment would not violate the applicable capital test (earned-surplus or impairment-of-capital, depending on the state), in nearly all states payment of a dividend is prohibited if it would leave the corporation insolvent.

2. Liability of Directors

If the directors approve a dividend at a time when the statute prohibits it, they may be personally liable. 승인하다

a) Bad Faith

If the directors know that the dividend is forbidden at the time they pay it, they are **personally liable** in nearly all states.

b) Negligence

If they act in good faith but are negligent in failing to notice that the dividend is forbidden, they are liable in some but probably not most states.

c) Creditor Suit

Usually, the suit to recover an improperly-paid dividend must be brought by the corporation (perhaps by means of a shareholder derivative suit, or by a trustee for the corporation once it declares bankruptcy). But some states allow suit to be brought by a creditor against the director(s) who approve an improper dividend.

가능성, 수단, 방법

3. Liability of Shareholders

A shareholder who receives an improper dividend may also be liable.

a) Common Law

At common law, the shareholder will be liable and required to return the improper dividend if either: (1) the corporation was insolvent at the time of, or as the result of the payment of the dividend; or (2) the shareholder knew, at the time he received the dividend, that it was improper. But if the corporation is solvent and the shareholder takes the dividend without notice that it violates the statute, **the shareholder does not have to return it at common law.**

b) Statute

Some corporation statutes make the shareholder liable to return the improper dividend, even if he would not be liable at common law. Apart from the basic corporation statute, the statute dealing with fraudulent conveyances (e.g., the Uniform Fraudulent Conveyance Act) may permit a creditor or bankruptcy trustee to recover against a shareholder.

부적절한

사기의, 기망의 / (부동산의) 양도

Diagram 24

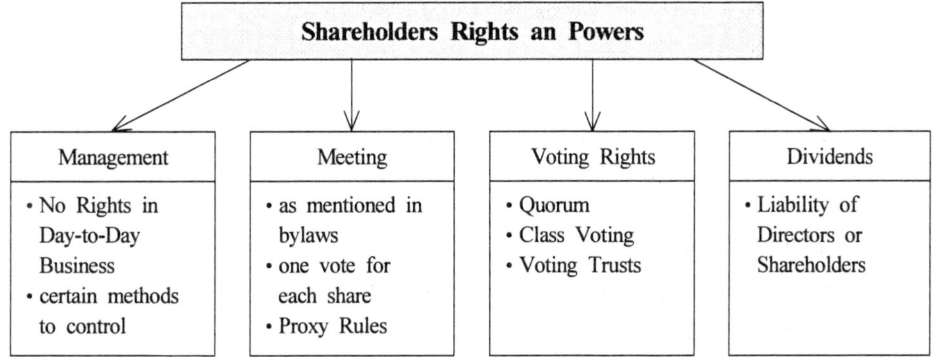

L. Resolution of Disputes

I. Dissension and Deadlock

The courts often have to deal with "dissension" and "deadlock" among the stockholders. "Dissension" refers to **squabbles or disagreements** among them. "Deadlock" refers to a situation where the **corporation is paralyzed and prevented from acting** (e.g., two factions each control the same number of directors, and the two factions cannot agree).

의견차이
절뚝거리는

II. Dissolution

The term dissolution as applied to a corporation signifies the termination of its corporate existence in any manner.

1. Kinds of Dissolution

There are two kinds of dissolution. It may be either de facto or de jure:

A **de jure dissolution** is one which is accomplished by judicial edict or decree, or which results from the expiration of the charter period of the corporate life.

달성하다

A **de facto dissolution**, on the other hand, occurs when the corporation, by reason of insolvency, cessation of business or otherwise, suspends all of its operations and goes into liquidation.

중단

This means the final winding up of its affairs, by getting its assets assembled, settling with creditors and debtors, and apportioning any profits or losses among the stockholders.

2. Grounds of Dissolution

Various legal grounds exist for the dissolution of a corporation, among which are:

- ▸ a fraudulent or **invalid corporation** 사기의
- ▸ the **expiration of the period** of existence provided for in the corporate charter
- ▸ **repeal by the legislature** of the corporate charter. However, some states do not reserve the right to repeal a charter, and, therefore, cannot exercise such power. 폐지, 인가취소
- ▸ the **failure of the primary purpose** of the corporation
- ▸ total non-use of the corporate franchise
- ▸ **willful and repeated misuse** of the corporate franchise or corporate power. In all such cases, however, some public interest must be involved before a dissolution will be directed. 남용
- ▸ a transfer by a corporation, voluntary or otherwise, of all of its rights and franchises, which by law, generally operates as a corporate dissolution

Most states hold that even if the statutory criteria are met, the judge still has discretion to refuse to award dissolution (e.g., when it would be unfair to one or more shareholders). 재량

Part 5: Limited Liability Company

Many states have promulgated statutes regulating another form of business organization: The Limited Liability Company ("L.L.C."). Small businesses are sometimes formed as an L.L.C., because this form tries to combine some of the advantages of both the partnership and the corporation. 공포하다

A. Purpose

An L.L.C. is an entity **designed to be taxed like a**

partnership but offers its owners, who are called members, the limited liability that shareholders of a corporation enjoy. Under current tax laws, unless an L.L.C. requests to be taxed as a corporation, it will receive partnership tax treatment (i.e., the L.L.C. will not be treated as a taxable entity; its profits and losses flow through the L.L.C. to its owners).

이익
손실

Although L.L.C.s are governed by statute, the statute provides that L.L.C. members can adopt operating agreements with provisions different from the L.L.C. statute, and generally the operating agreements will control.

An L.L.C. is treated as an entity distinct from its members. It may hold property in its own name, sue or be sued, etc.

B. Formation

In New York for example, an L.L.C. is formed by **filing articles of organization with the department of state.** An L.L.C. must have at least two members.

I. Contents of Articles

The articles of organization of an L.L.C. must include the following:

- ▸ The **name of** the L.L.C., which must contain the words "Limited Liability Company" or the abbreviations "L.L.C." or "LLC"; — 약어, 축약어
- ▸ The **county** within the state where its principal place of business is to be located; — 주 사업지 주소, 본사 주소
- ▸ The **date of its dissolution** if the term is not perpetual;
- ▸ Designation of the department of state for service of process;
- ▸ Whether the L.L.C. is to be managed by one or more members, a class of members, or one or more managers;
- ▸ Whether any member or members are to be liable for all or certain specified debts of the L.L.C.; and
- ▸ A general or specific purpose clause.

II. Publication

A summary of the articles of organization must be published once a week for six consecutive weeks in two newspapers, one of which must be a newspaper published in the city or town in which the L.L.C. has its principal place of business. Proof of publication must be filed with the department of state within 120 days of the date the articles of organization are effective. Failure to file proof of publication within the prescribed time will prohibit the L.L.C. from maintaining an action in New York until such time as the requirement is complied with.

III. Management

Management of the L.L.C. is **presumed to be by all members.** Other management arrangements can be made (e.g., management by only some of the members or by outside managers), but they must be specified in the articles. If management is by the members: (i) a majority vote is required to approve most decisions and (ii) each member is an agent of the L.L.C. (i.e., the L.L.C. may be bound by the acts of any member). 전제하다, 추정하다

C. Liability of Members

As indicated above, **members are not personally liable for the L.L.C.'s obligations** unless otherwise indicated in the articles of organization.

D. Sharing Profits and Losses

Profits and losses of an L.L.C. are allocated on the basis of contributions, unless otherwise provided in the operating agreement. 배분하다

E. Transfers of Interest

An assignment of a member's interest in an L.L.C. 양도

transfers only the member's right to receive profits and losses. Management rights are not transferred. One can become a member (i.e., management rights can be transferred) only with the consent of all members.

F. Dissolution

Disassociation (e.g., death, retirement, resignation, bankruptcy, or incompetence) of an L.L.C. member generally causes dissolution of the L.L.C. 은퇴, 퇴직

Further reading

Ribstein/Mason/Letsou, Business Associations (3rd ed., 1996); *Gerber*, Business Reorganizations (3rd ed.); *Hynes*, Agency, Partnership an the LLC (6th ed., 1999); *Clark*, Corporate Law (1986); *Henn/Alexander*, Handbook of the Law of Corporations and Other Business Enterprises (1983); *Klein/Coffee*, Business Organisation and Finance; *Romano*, Foundations of Corporate Law (1993); *Reuschlein/Gregory*, The Law of Agency and Partnership (1990).

Chapter Seven

Procedural Questions

Part 1: Introduction

The U.S. court system is divided into two separate branches: The **state courts** and the **federal courts**. Therefore, procedural questions in the United States have always to deal with this division. If a case comes up, there is always at first the question if it should be brought before a federal or a state court. After this question has been answered, the applicable law has to be determined.

가지, 하위종류

준거법

Since the purpose of this chapter is to get a broad idea about U.S. procedural law, it will mainly deal with the federal procedural law.

Part 2: Federal Courts

A. Structure

The U.S. Constitution provides for an explicit structure of a federal court system.

규정하다

I. Supreme Court

The Supreme Court is the **highest court** in the federal judiciary. Chapter One of the First Volume already described it.

연방법원의 체계

II. Trial Courts

The United States **district courts are the trial courts** of the federal system. Within limits set by Congress and the Constitution, the district courts have jurisdiction to hear

(광의의) 관할권

nearly all categories of federal cases, including both civil and criminal matters. There are 94 federal judicial districts, including at least one district in each state.

III. Appellate Courts

The **94 judicial districts** are organized into **12 regional circuits**, each of which has a United States court of appeals. A court of appeals hears appeals from the district courts located within its circuit, as well as appeals from decisions of federal administrative agencies. In addition, the Court of Appeals for the Federal Circuit has nationwide jurisdiction to hear appeals in specialized cases, such as those involving patent laws and cases decided by the Court of International Trade.

항소법원

국제무역

Diagram 25

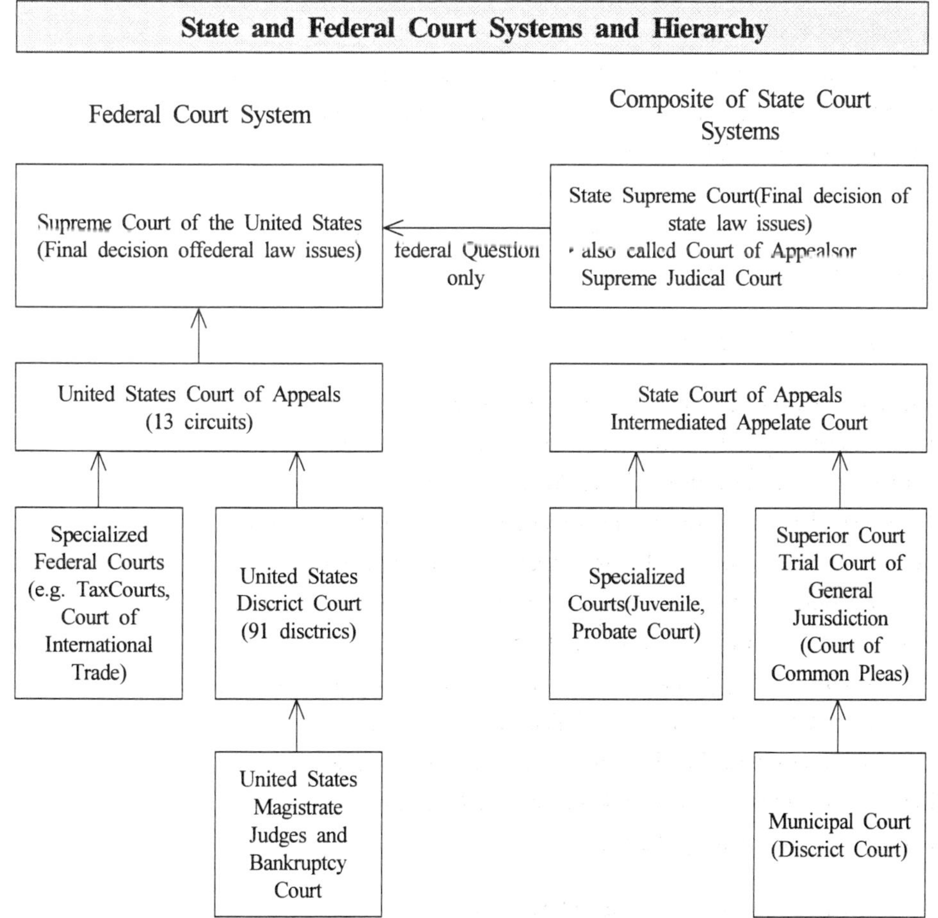

B. Judicial Process

This section describes three key features of the federal judicial system and gives an overview of the process in criminal cases, civil cases, and bankruptcy proceedings. 특징

I. An Adversarial System

The litigation process in United States courts is referred to as an "**adversarial**" **system because it relies on the litigants to present their dispute before a neutral fact-finder**. According to American legal tradition, inherited from the English common law, the clash of adversaries before the court is most likely to allow the jury or judge to determine the truth and resolve the dispute at hand. In some other legal systems, judges or other court officials investigate and assist the parties to find relevant evidence or obtain testimony from witnesses. In the United States, the work of collecting evidence and preparing to present it to the court is accomplished by the litigants and their attorneys, normally without assistance from the court.

적대관계에 있는
상속하다
조사하다
증거
변호사

II. Fees and Costs of Litigation

Another characteristic of the American judicial system is that litigants typically pay their own court costs and attorney's fees whether they win or lose. The federal courts charge fees that are mostly set by Congress. For example, it costs US $150 to file a civil case. Other costs of litigation, such as attorneys and expert fees, are more substantial.

비용

In criminal cases the government pays the costs of investigation and prosecution. The government also provides a lawyer without cost for any criminal defendant who is unable to afford one. In civil cases, plaintiffs who cannot afford to pay court fees may seek permission from the court to proceed without paying those fees.

형사소추

III. Procedural Rules for conduct of Litigation

There are federal **rules of evidence**, and rules of civil, criminal and appellate procedure that must be followed in the federal courts. They are designed to promote simplicity, fairness, the just determination of litigation, and the elimination of unjustifiable expense and delay. The rules are drafted by committees of judges, lawyers, and professors appointed by the Chief Justice.

증거법

(미연방) 대법원장

C. Civil Cases

A federal civil case involves a **legal dispute between at least two parties**. To begin a civil lawsuit in federal court, the plaintiff files a complaint with the court and "serves" a copy of the complaint on the defendant. The complaint describes the plaintiff's injury, explains how the defendant caused the injury, and asks the court to order relief. A plaintiff may seek money to compensate for the injury, or may ask the court to order the defendant to stop the conduct that is causing the harm.

소

I. Discovery

To prepare a case for trial, the litigants may conduct "discovery". In discovery, the **litigants must provide information to each other about the case**, such as the identity of witnesses and copies of any document related to the case. The purpose of discovery is to prepare for trial by requiring the litigants to assemble their evidence and prepare to call witnesses. Each side also may file requests, or "motions", with the court seeking rulings on the discovery of evidence, or on the procedure to be followed at trial.

디스커버리, 증거자료의 공개

증인

요구

1. Deposition

One common method of discovery is the deposition. In a deposition, a witness is required to answer under oath questions about the case asked by the lawyers in the presence of a court reporter. The court reporter is a person specially trained to record all testimony and produce a word-for-word account called a transcript.

선거증서

(법정) 선서

Brandenberg v. El Al Israel Airlines – 79 FRD 543 (SDNY 1978)

Brandenberg was a 72-year-old woman who flew abroad to visit her daughter and was carried by British Airways. Brandenberg apparently was very critical of her service during the flight.

The plaintiff brought a $900,000 negligence action against the defendant, alleging physical stress and mental injuries, and that because she was old, the airline had a duty to treat her with particular care, and they had breached that duty, "abandoning her in her time of need." During discovery, the plaintiff was advised not to answer several questions that asked her the basis of her claim. Defendant moved under Rule 37(a) to compel answers.

포기하다, 떠나다

강요하다

Issue

Whether a plaintiff may properly refuse to answer any question during deposition which asks for the basis of the plaintiff's claim.

Holding and Reasoning

No. The defendant is left in the dark by the pleadings and her refusal to answer these questions as to the factual basis of her claim of negligence. The defendant is entitled to discover the facts underlying the claim, and so the plaintiff must answer them.

준비서면

II. Alternative Dispute Resolution

To avoid the expense and delay of having a trial, judges encourage the litigants to try to **reach an agreement resolving their dispute**. In particular, the courts encourage the use of mediation, arbitration, and other forms of alternative dispute resolution (ADR), designed to produce an early resolution of a dispute without the need for trial or other court proceedings. As a result, litigants often decide to resolve a civil lawsuit with an agreement known as a "settlement".

1심판결
독려하다
중재
화해, 화의

III. Trial

If a case is not settled, the court will schedule a trial. In a wide variety of civil cases, either side is entitled under the Constitution to request a jury trial. If the parties waive their right to a jury, then the case will be heard by a judge without a jury. 포기하다

1. Principles of Conduct

At a trial, **witnesses testify under the supervision of a judge.** By applying rules of evidence, the judge determines which information may be presented in the courtroom. To ensure that witnesses speak from their own knowledge and do not change the story based on what they hear another witness say, witnesses are kept out of the courtroom until it is time for them to testify. A court reporter keeps a record of the trial proceedings. A deputy clerk of court also keeps a record of each person who testifies and marks for the record any documents, photographs, or other items introduced into evidence. 감독 결정하다

2. Objections

As the questioning of a witness proceeds, the opposing attorney may object to a question if it invites the witness to say something that is not based on the witness's personal knowledge, is unfairly prejudicial, or is irrelevant to the case. The judge rules on the objection, generally by ruling that it is either **sustained** or **overruled**. If the objection is sustained, the witness is not required to answer the question, and the attorney must move on to his next question. The court reporter records the objections so that a court of appeals can review the arguments later if necessary. 반대편의 이의를 제기하다 인용하다 / 기각하다 항소법원

3. Final Stage

At the conclusion of the evidence, each side gives a closing argument. In a jury trial, the **judge will explain the law that is relevant to the case** and the decisions the jury needs to make. The jury generally is asked to determine whether the defendant is responsible for harming the plaintiff in some way, and then to determine the amount of damages that the defendant will be required to pay. If the case is being tried before a judge without a jury, known as a "**bench trial**", the judge will decide these issues. In a civil case the plaintiff must convince the jury by a "**preponderance of the evidence**" that the defendant is responsible for the harm the plaintiff has suffered. 확신시키다

D. Criminal Cases

The judicial process in a criminal case differs from a civil case in several important ways. At the beginning of a federal criminal case, the principal actors are the U.S. attorney (the prosecutor) and the **grand jury**. The U.S. attorney represents the United States in most court proceedings, including all criminal prosecutions. The grand jury reviews evidence presented by the U.S. attorney and decides whether there is sufficient evidence to require a defendant to stand trial. 검사

I. Pretrial Interrogation

After a person is arrested, a **pretrial service or probation officer of the court immediately interviews the defendant** and conducts an investigation of the defendant's background. The information obtained by the pretrial services or probation office will be used to help a judge decide whether to release the defendant into the community before trial, and whether to impose conditions to release. 집행유예 감독관

II. Initial Appearance

At an initial appearance, a judge advises the defendant of the charges filed, considers whether the defendant should be held in jail until trial, and determines whether there is probable cause to believe that an offense has been committed and the defendant has committed it. Defendants who are unable to afford counsel are advised of their right to a 범죄

court-appointed attorney. The court may appoint either a federal public defender or a private attorney who has agreed to accept such appointments from the court. In either type of appointment, the attorney will be paid by the court from funds appropriated by Congress. Defendants released into the community before trial may be required to obey certain restrictions, such as home confinement or drug testing, and to make periodic reports to a pretrial services officer to ensure appearance at trial.

재택연금

III. Arraignment

The **defendant enters a plea** to the charges brought by the U.S. attorney at a hearing known as an arraignment. Most defendants plead guilty rather than go to trial. If a defendant pleads guilty in return for the government agreeing to drop certain charges or to recommend a lenient sentence, the **agreement often is called a "plea bargain"**. If the defendant pleads guilty, the judge may impose a sentence at that time, but more commonly will schedule a hearing to determine the sentence at a later date. In most felony cases the judge waits for the results of a presentence report, prepared by the court's probate office, before imposing sentence. If the defendant pleads not guilty, the judge will proceed to schedule a trial.

방어변론

인자한, 관대한 / 판결

중범죄

IV. Burden of Proof

In a criminal case, the burden of proof is on the government. Defendants do not have to prove their innocence. Instead, the government must provide evidence to convince the jury of the defendant's guilt. The standard of proof in a criminal trial is proof "beyond a reasonable doubt", which means the evidence must be so strong that there is no reasonable doubt that the defendant committed the crime.

무죄

V. Result of the Verdict: Not Guilty

If a defendant is found **not guilty**, **the defendant is released** and the government may not appeal. Nor can the person be charged again with the same crime in a federal court. The constitution prohibits **"double jeopardy"** or being tried twice for the same offense. 중복처벌을 금지하다

VI. Result of the Verdict: Guilty

If the verdict is guilty, the judge determines the defendant's sentence according to special federal sentencing guidelines issued by the United States Sentencing Commission. The court's probation office prepares a report for the court that applies the sentencing guidelines to the individual defendant and the crimes for which he has been found guilty. During sentencing, the court may consider not only the evidence produced at trial, but all relevant information that may be provided by the pretrial service officer, the U.S. attorney, and the defense attorney.

A sentence may include **time in prison**, a **fine to be paid** to the government, and **restitution to be paid to crime victims**. The court's probation officers assist the court in enforcing any conditions that are imposed as part of a criminal sentence. The supervision of offenders also may involve services such as substance abuse testing and treatment programs. 감옥 / 벌금형

E. The Appeals Process

The losing party in a decision by a trial court in the federal system normally is entitled to appeal the decision to a federal court of appeals.

I. Trial Court Actions that are Reviewable

In a civil case either side may appeal the verdict. In a criminal case, the defendant may appeal a guilty verdict, but the government may not appeal if a defendant is found not guilty. Either side in a criminal case may appeal with respect to the sentence that is imposed after a guilty verdict.

1. Interlocutory Appeals

Appeals of non-final orders, called "interlocutory appeals," 임시의

are often allowed, but they are discretionary. Usually both the trial court and the appellate court must agree that the issue raised by the interlocutory order is a close one and that it would be efficient to address the issue without waiting for a final judgment. 재량에 달린

There are a few other exceptions to the final judgment requirement, primarily based on overriding need to have the issue addressed at an early stage of the litigation.

2. Mandamus

A limited path around the final judgment rule may be reached by two forms of action. One is an action for a "writ of mandamus". This is an **order requiring certain trial court action**. The other is an action for a "writ of prohibition", which is an **order prohibiting certain trial court action**.

These forms of action avoid the final judgment rule because they are considered to be an original action filed against the trial judge (often by name) rather than an appeal. The limited nature of mandamus review must be emphasized, however. In the federal system, at least, the occasions for mandamus are narrow and it is said that "mandamus will not lie" for any error that could be remedied adequately by appeal.

II. Grounds

A litigant who files an appeal, known as an **appellant**, must show that the trial court made a **legal error that affected the decision in the case**. The court of appeals makes its decision based on the record of the case established by the trial court. It does not receive additional evidence or hear witnesses. The court of appeals also may review the factual findings of the trial court, but typically may only overturn a decision on factual grounds if the findings were "clearly erroneous". 항소심의 원고 / 증거 / 증인

III. Panel's Decision

Appeals are decided by panels of three judges working 재판부

together. The **appellant presents legal arguments** to the panel, in writing, in a **document called a "brief"**. In the brief the appellant tries to persuade the judges that the trial court made an error, and that its decision should be reversed. On the other hand, the party defending against the appeal, known as the "appellee", tries in its brief to show why the trial court decision was correct, or why any error made by the trial court was not significant enough to affect the outcome of the case.

항소심의 피고

결론, 결과

Although some cases are decided on the basis of written briefs alone, many cases are selected for an "oral argument" before the court. Oral argument in the court of appeals is a structured discussion between the appellate lawyers and the penal of judges focusing on the legal principles in dispute.

IV. Supreme Court

The court of appeals decision usually will be the final word in the case, unless it sends the case back to the trial court for additional proceedings, or the parties ask the U.S. Supreme Court to review the case. In some cases the decisions may be reviewed en banc, that is, by a larger group of judges of the court of appeals for the circuit.

There are two ways to seek review by the U.S. Supreme Court: **an appeal as a matter of right and the discretionary grant of a writ of certiorari**. Very few cases fall into the category of appeals as of right, so as a practical matter certiorari is the only way to gain Supreme Court review.

Certiorari means to "bring up the record," generally the first step in an appeal to any appellate court once jurisdiction is taken. By exercising its appellate certiorari jurisdiction over cases involving issues of federal law coming from the lower federal courts and the highest courts of the states, the Court maintains the supremacy and consistency of federal law.

관할

우선권 / 일치, 일관성

Part 3: The Jury

Perhaps the most important way individuals become involved in the U.S. federal judicial process is by serving as a juror. There are two types of juries serving distinct functions in the federal trial courts: **trial juries**, and **grand juries**. 배심원

A. Civil Trial Jury

The **Seventh Amendment** to the U.S. Constitution says that

> *"in suits at common law ... the right of trial by jury shall be preserved..."*

This Amendment applies to federal trials, but does not apply to state trials.

I. Number of Jurors

Traditionally, juries have been composed of **12 members**. But this has changed in the past.

Even in federal civil cases, the Seventh Amendment does not require a 12-member jury. Rule 48 of the Federal Rules of Civil Procedure provides that a jury of at least six members will be seated.

Normally the federal court seats more than six jurors, so that if some have to leave the panel, there will be at least six at the time of verdict. If there are fewer than six at the time of verdict, the court must declare a mistrial unless both parties agree to continue. 배심평결 (소송법상) 하자있는 재판

The number of jurors in state trials varies from state to state.

II. Unanimity

The **verdict** of a federal civil jury **must be unanimous**, unless the parties stipulate otherwise. Most states allow a less-than-unanimous civil verdict. 만장일치로

III. Jury Selection

The process by which the jury is selected is called the "voir dire." In most states, the voir dire consists of oral questions by both sides' counsel to the prospective jurors. These questions are designed to discover whether a juror would be biased, or has connections with a party or prospective witness. 편향된

1. Dismissal for Cause

Any juror who is shown through the voir dire to be biased or connected to the case must be dismissed upon motion by a party (dismissal "for cause"). There is no limit to the number of for-cause challenges by either party.

2. Challenges Without Cause

In addition to the jurors dismissed for cause, each party may dismiss a certain number of other prospective jurors without showing cause for their dismissal (**"peremptory challenges"**). (이유를 밝히지 않고) 특정한 배심원을 거부하다

3. Balanced Pool

The Seventh Amendment requires that the jury, and the pool from which it is drawn, be roughly representative of the overall community.

4. Alternates

In most states, the court orders the selection of up to **six alternates** after the "regular" members of the jury have been selected. But under federal practice, alternates are no longer used. 예비자(명단)

5. Instructions

The judge must instruct the jury as to the relevant law. 지시하다

A party who wants to raise the inadequacy of the instructions on appeal must object to those instructions before the jury retires. (Sometimes courts make an exception to this rule for "plain error.")

6. Juror Misconduct

A jury verdict may be set aside, and a new trial ordered, for certain types of jury misconduct. (Examples: Talking to a party, receiving a bribe, concealing a bias on voir dire.) 비행 뇌물

B. Criminal Trial Jury

A criminal jury trial is usually made up of **12 members**. Criminal juries decide whether the defendant committed the crime as charged. The sentence usually is set by a judge. Verdicts in both civil and criminal cases must be unanimous, although the parties in a civil case may agree to a non-unanimous verdict. A jury's deliberations are conducted in private, out of sight and hearing of the judge, litigants, witnesses, and others in the courtroom. 심의, 토의 재판 당사자들 증인

C. Grand Jury

A grand jury, which normally consists of **15 to 23 members**, has a more specialized function. The U.S. attorney, the prosecutor in federal criminal cases, presents evidence to the grand jury for them to determine whether there is "probable cause" to believe that an individual has committed a crime and should be put on trial. If the grand jury decides there is enough evidence, it will issue an indictment against the defendant. Grand jury proceedings are not open for public observation. 기소장

Part 4: Jurisdiction

A court can only try a case, if it has jurisdiction over it. Before an action is commenced there are certain questions that must be answered:

- Does the court have jurisdiction over the defendant (in **personam jurisdiction**)? 피고

- Does the **court have jurisdiction** over the property in question (in rem jurisdiction)? 소유권
- Was the defendant given proper service, reasonable notice and an opportunity to be heard? 송달
- Does the court have the competency to hear the case and issue a judgement (**subject matter jurisdiction**)?
- Is the case being tried in the proper **venue**?
- If the case is brought in federal court, what is the applicable law?

A. Personal Jurisdiction

Under personal jurisdiction there are three different kinds of jurisdiction which a court may exercise over the parties— one of these three must be present:

- **In personam jurisdiction**, or jurisdiction over the defendant's "person," gives the court power to issue a judgment against him personally. Thus all of the person's assets may be seized to satisfy the judgment, and the judgment can be sued upon in other states as well. 재산 / 압류하다
- In rem jurisdiction, or jurisdiction over a thing, gives the court power to adjudicate a claim made about a piece of property or about a status. 판결을 내리다
- In **quasi in rem jurisdiction**, the action has begun by seizing property owned by (attachment), or a debt owed to (garnishment) the defendant, within the forum state. The thing seized is a pretext for the court to decide the case without having jurisdiction over the defendant's person. Any judgment affects only the property seized, and the judgment cannot be sued upon in any other court. 압류 채권압류

If jurisdiction in the case is in personam or quasi in rem, the court may not exercise that jurisdiction unless defendan thas "**minimum contacts**" with the state in which the court sits. In brief, the requirement of minimum contacts means that defendant has to have taken actions that were purposefully directed towards the forum state.

Most states have "**long-arm statutes.**" A long-arm statute is a statute which permits the court of a state to obtain jurisdiction over persons not physically present within the state at the time of service.

I. In Personam Jurisdiction

In most states, there are a number of different criteria which will enable the court to take personal jurisdiction over an individual. Some of the most common (each of which will be considered in detail below) are:

- **Presence** within the forum state;
- **Domicile** or residence within the forum state; 주소
- **Consent** to be sued within the forum state;
- **Driving a car** within the forum state;
- Committing a **tortious act** within the state (or, perhaps, committing an out-of-state act with in-state tortious consequences);
- Ownership of **property** in the forum state;
- **Conducting business** in the forum state;
- Being **married** in, or living while married in, the forum state.

1. Presence

Presence is the traditional requirement for in personam jurisdiction.

Jurisdiction may be exercised over an individual by virtue of his **presence within the forum state**. That is, even if the individual is an out-of-state resident who comes into the forum state only briefly, personal jurisdiction over him may be gotten as long as service was made on him while he was in the forum state. ~에 근거하여

Burnham v. Superior Court – 495 US 604 (1990)

Burnham and his wife separated in New Jersey, and she took their children to California. Burnham continued to reside in New Jersey, but made a few visits to California for 분가하다, 별거하다

business, and to visit his children. During one of those visits, he was served with divorce papers by his wife.

Burnham made a special appearance to quash service on the grounds of lack of personal jurisdiction due to insufficient "minimum contacts." The California court held that physical presence in the state combined with personal service was a sufficient basis for jurisdiction, regardless of the level of contacts Burnham had with the state.

Issue

Whether the "minimum contacts" requirement of International Shoe (see infra p.175) precludes a state from acquiring in personam jurisdiction over a non- resident defendant who is personally served while transiently physically present within the state.

배제하다, 제외하다

일시적인

Holding and Reasoning

No. [Scalia] International Shoe merely served to cast aside the fictions of consent and presence of a non-present non-resident, holding that due process does not necessarily require the states to adhere to the unbending territorial limits on jurisdiction as set forth in Pennoyer (see supra p. 172). "Minimum contacts" may take the place of physical presence. However, it is illogical to assume that now physical presence is not sufficient. It is traditional that physical presence be sufficient, and so it satisfies due process. There is no need to apply any contemporary due process analysis to physical presence basis for jurisdiction, because it is validated by its own pedigree.

동시대의

출신, 출처, 혈통

2. Domicile

Jurisdiction may be exercised over a person who is domiciled within the forum state, even if the person is temporarily absent from the state. A person is considered to be domiciled in the place where he has his current dwelling place, if he also has the intention to remain in that place for an indefinite period.

거주하다

3. Residence

Some states allow jurisdiction to be exercised on the basis of defendant's residence in the forum state, even though he is absent from the state. A person may have several residences simultaneously.

4. Consent

Jurisdiction over a party can be exercised by virtue of her consent, even if she has no contacts whatsoever with the forum state.

5. Non-resident Motorist

Most states have statutes allowing the courts to exercise jurisdiction over non-resident motorists who have been involved in accidents in the state.

6. In-state Tortious Conduct

Many states have statutes allowing their courts jurisdiction over persons committing tortious acts within the state.

Some **"in-state tortious acts" long-arm clauses** have been interpreted to include acts done outside the state which produce tortious consequences within the state. In a products liability situation, a vendor who sells products that he knows will be used in the state may constitutionally be required to defend in the state, if the product causes injury in the state.

매도인

Gray v. American Radiator & Standard Sanitary Corp., – 176 NE.2d 761 (1961)

The plaintiff was injured by an exploding water heater in Illinois. The water heater was assembled in Pennsylvania by the defendant, and the valve that exploded was manufactured in Ohio by Titan. The water heater was sold in Illinois. Titan had no contacts in the state of Illinois except that its valves were used on water heaters sold to customers there.

조립하다
밸브

The defendant cross-claimed against Titan for indemnifica-

반소를 제기하다

tion under warranties. Titan moved to dismiss the claim and the cross-claim for lack of jurisdiction over the person. The trial court granted the motion, and the plaintiff appeals.

Issue

1. Whether a tortious act was committed in Illinois within the meaning of the Illinois jurisdictional (long-arm) statute, and

2. whether the statute, if so constructed, was consistent with due process.

Holding and Reasoning

Yes. Although the valve was manufactured out of state, a "tortious act" plainly refers to conduct that results in an injury, thus being inseparable from the injury itself. Thus, the place of the wrong is the last place where an event takes place which is necessary to render the actor liable. Here, that was the explosion which occurred in Illinois. Also, since the statute of limitations is measured from the time of the injury, 시효 then it makes sense to fix the place of the tortious act in the place of the injury. There is legislative history indicating that the legislature meant to go to the limits of the due process clause. With regard to due process, it is a reasonable inference that Titan's valves are frequently and substantially used in the state of Illinois. As such, there is sufficient basis for jurisdiction.

7. Owners of in-state Property

Many states exercise jurisdiction over owners of in-state property in causes of action arising from that property.

8. Conducting Business

States often exercise jurisdiction over non-residents who **conduct businesses within the state**. Since states may regulate an individual's business conduct in the state, they may constitutionally exercise jurisdiction relating to that doing of business.

9. Domestic Relations Cases

Courts sometimes try to take personal jurisdiction over a non-resident party to a domestic relations case. However, the requirement of "minimum contacts" applies here (as in every personal jurisdiction situation), and that requirement may bar the state from taking jurisdiction. 하지 못하게 막다

II. In Rem Jurisdiction

The court has jurisdiction over a defendant, if defendant owns property inside the state and this property is under dispute between the parties. 분쟁중인

One important type of in rem action is an action for specific performance of a contract to convey land. Even if the defendant is out of state and has no connection with the forum state other than having entered into a contract to convey in-state land, the forum state may hear the action; defendant does not have to have minimum contacts with the forum state for the action to proceed – it is enough that the contract involved in-state land, and that defendant has received reasonable notice. 토지소유권을 이전하다

III. Quasi in Rem Jurisdiction

A quasi in rem action is one that would have been in personam if jurisdiction over defendant's person had been attainable. Instead, property or intangibles are seized not as the object of the litigation, but merely as a means of satisfying a possible judgment against the defendant. A case where this rule first was recognized was Pennoyer v. Neff, 95 U.S. 714 (1877). In this case, the Supreme Court also gave the territorial approach constitutional approval. Additionally, it set forth standards for other questions concerning personal jurisdiction. 얻을 수 있는 / 무형의 재산

Furthermore, quasi in rem jurisdiction over defendant cannot be exercised unless defendant had such "minimum contacts" with the forum state that in personam jurisdiction could be exercised over him. This is the holding of the landmark case of Shaffer v. Heitner.

Shaffer v. Heitner – 433 U.S. 186 (1977)

Heitner is a stockholder of Greyhound Lines, and Shaffer is an officer of Greyhound who has a large amount of stock. Apparently, Greyhound lost an anti-trust suit and was held liable for a large criminal contempt judgment. Greyhound is a Delaware corporation with its principal place of business in Arizona. None of its officers are residents of Delaware. Delaware has a statute that provides that stock of Delaware corporations is located in Delaware. Delaware also has a quasi-in rem jurisdictional statute that allows a plaintiff to attach in-state property in order to compel a general appearance by the defendant.

주주

주민

압류하다

Heitner brought a stockholder derivative suit in Delaware state court, and seized a large amount of stock of Greyhound belonging to the defendant officers. All of the defendant officers were served by certified mail. Defendants made a special appearance to quash service and free their assets, but the trial court denied. The Delaware state supreme court affirmed jursidiction, holding that the "minimum contacts" requirement of International Shoe did not apply because they were exercising quasi in-rem jurisdiction and not in personam jurisdiction.

Issue

Whether the standard of fairness and substantial justice set forth in International Shoe should be held to govern quasi in rem actions as well as in personam actions.

Holding and Reasoning

Yes. Pennoyer's territorial boundary test, which provided for quasi in rem jurisdiction solely due to the presence of property in the state (because it only "indirectly" affected the rights of the person), is outmoded. It also leads to arguments over whether the action is one in personam or quasi in rem. Since an in rem or quasi in rem action is really just a proceeding against the rights of a person, and therefore

경계

낡은, 낡아서 유효하지 않은

against the person himself, it should also be subject to the International Shoe minimum contacts standard. Of course, the presence of property in the state may bear on the existence of minimum contacts, especially where the underlying claim arises from the existence of the property. Thus, many in rem actions and quasi in rem type of actions would not be affected by requiring minimum contacts. However, for quasi in rem type of actions, such as that in Harris v. Balk, the presence of property alone would not support jurisdiction absent other ties to the state. This does not allow a defendant to avoid payment of his obligations by moving his property out of state, because the plaintiff could still obtain a judgment in another state and it would be valid in the state where defendant's property lies under the Full Faith and Credit clause. Lastly, these officers do not have minimum contacts with Delaware because they have never been there and only own property there because of the statute. They can not be said to have implied consent to submit to in personam jurisdiction. The state does not acquire jursidiction over a non-resident just because it is the center of gravity of the litigation. Any interests that Delaware has in controlling its corporations are only of concern for choice of law, not for determination of in personam jurisdiction.

청구, 청구권

~이 없으므로 / 관련, 연결

얻다

중대함

IV. Jurisdiction over Corporations

Any action may be brought against a domestic corporation, i.e., **one which is incorporated in the forum state**. A state is much more limited in its ability to exercise jurisdiction over a foreign corporation (i.e., a corporation not incorporated in the forum state).

내국의

1. Minimum Contacts

The forum state may exercise personal jurisdiction over the corporation only if the corporation has "**minimum contacts**" with the forum state "such that the maintenance of the suit does not offend 'traditional notions of fair play and substantial justice.'"

International Shoe Co. v. Washington – 326 US 310 (1945)

The shoe company is a Delaware corporation, with its principal place of business in Missiouri. It "employs" several salesmen in the state of Washington, who solicit orders for shoes, which are in turn shipped into Washington. The salesman is paid a commission. Washington had an unemployment compensation statute which required employers doing business in the state to pay a certain percentage into the fund on a per-employee basis. The shoe company did not pay this amount, claiming that the tax was a burden on interstate commerce, and a violation of the 14th amendment.

사업지 주소
노력하다, 애쓰다

The state served notice on a salesman who resided in Washington, and also mailed a copy to the shoe company at its Missouri address [as required by the statute]. The shoe company appealed all the way to the Supreme Court, with each lower court finding that it had sufficient activity in the state to be considered amenable to suit there.

살다, 거주하다
항소를 제기하다
(가능성이) 열려있는

Issue

Whether the shoe company has sufficient activity in the state of Washington to render itself amenable to suit there.

Holding and Reasoning

Yes. First, the tax is not a burden on interstate commerce because the states have power under federal statute to make foreign corporations doing business in the state subject to the unemployment tax. In order to determine whether a business has sufficient in-state presence for nexus purposes to satisfy the due process clause, an "estimate of the inconveniences" which would result to the corporation from a trial away from its "home" or principal place of business is relevant. Whether due process is satisfied must depend on the quality and nature of the activity in relation to the fair and orderly administration of the laws which it was the purpose of the due process clause to insure. But to the extent a corporation exercises the privileges of conducting activities within a state,

핵심, 중심
불편함

it enjoys the protection of the laws of that state, and the right to bring actions in a court of that state. This gives rise to obligations at least as far as they arise out of the business conducted in the state. Thus, a procedure which requires the corporation to respond to a suit brought to enforce these obligations is not undue. Here, the activity was sufficient because it extended over a long time and was systematic, resulting in a large amount of product being shipped into the state. 보호

2. Dealings With Residents of Forum State

Usually, a corporation will be found to have the requisite "minimum contacts" with the forum state only if the corporation has somehow voluntarily sought to do business in, or with the residents of, the forum state. 필요한

3. Product Liability

The requirement of "minimum contacts" with the forum state leads to difficulties in product liability cases.

The mere fact that a product manufactured or sold by the defendant outside of the forum state and the product somehow finds its way into the forum state and causes injury there is not enough to subject the defendant to personal jurisdiction there. Instead, the defendant can be sued in the forum state only if it made some effort to market in the forum state, either directly or indirectly.

World-Wide Volkswagen Corp. v. Woodson – 444 US 286 (1980)

Plaintiffs purchased an Audi in New York from a local retailer. Plaintiffs were badly injured when the car exploded upon being hit from the rear during a trip through Oklahoma. The local retailer and his distributor do no business in Oklahoma. Their only connection with Oklahoma was that they sold the car to the plaintiffs who had an accident there. 소매상 중간상인, 도매인

Plaintiffs brought a products liability action against all members of the manufacture and distribution chain of the car 유통고리

under an Oklahoma Long Arm statute which provides for in personam jurisdiction over a non-resident if they cause tortious injury in the state "by act or omission outside this state" and if he "derives substantial revenue from goods used or consumed" in the state. The defendants made a special appearance to object to jurisdiction, but their motion was denied. The Plaintiffs argument was that it was foreseeable that the car would be driven in Oklahoma (because it is mobile), and that the defendant derived substantial revenu from cars driven in Oklahoma.

부작위
수익
외양
예측가능성

Issue

Whether sufficient basis exists to subject the defendants to in personam jurisdiction in Oklahoma consistent with due process.

Holding and Reasoning

No. The minimum contacts rule of due process serves two functions: it prevents unfair burdening of the defendant, and it ensures that the states do not reach out beyond their authority. It must be reasonable to subject the defendant to in personam jurisdiction in the forum court. The burden on the defendant, the state's interests, the plaintiff's interests, and the shared federal interest of the other states are all relevant factors. Although the expansion of personal jurisdiction has progressed, it has not gone so far as to apply to a person who has no contacts with the state. Here, the defendants have absolutely no contacts whatsoever. Mere foreseeability of injury in the forum state is insufficient because that would in effect make every seller amenable to suit wherever the chattel travelled, by unilateral activity, resulting in extreme unpredictability. That is not to say that a manufacturer who delivers products into the stream of commerce with the expectation that they will be consumed in the forum state is immune, but that is not the case here. There was no reason to believe that the defendants sought to receive any protection under the Oklahoma laws, or any revenue from sales of cars used in Oklahoma.

동산
예측불가능성

But if the out-of-state manufacturer makes or sells a product that it knows will be eventually sold in the forum state, this fact by itself is probably enough to establish minimum contacts. However, if this is the only contact that exists, it may nonetheless be "unreasonable" to make defendant defend there, and thus violate due process.

4. Unreasonableness

As the case in the above example shows, even where minimum contacts exist, it will be a **violation of due process** for the court to hear a case against a non-resident defendant where it would be "unreasonable" for the suit to be heard. The more burdensome it is to the defendant to have to litigate the case in the forum state, and the slimmer the contacts (though "minimum") with the forum state, the more likely this result is to occur.

5. Class Action Plaintiffs

An "absent" plaintiff in a class action that takes place in the forum state may be bound by the decision in the case, even if that plaintiff did not have minimum contacts with the forum state.

C. Subject Matter Jurisdiction

For a court properly to undertake a civil adjudication, the court must have, under applicable constitutional and statutory provisions, authority to **adjudicate the type of controversy before the court** – that is, it must have jurisdiction over the subject matter. 판결

1. State Courts

A state court of general jurisdiction can hear any case including those based entirely on federal law, unless Congress has made federal jurisdiction exclusive.

A state may organize its judicial branch as it wishes. A state has considerable freedom in allocating jurisdiction to its courts of original and appellate jurisdiction, subject to occasional federal statutes excluding state courts from certain subject areas.

1. General Versus Limited Jurisdiction

Typically, a state's courts of original jurisdiction include one set of courts of general jurisdiction, which can hear any type of action not specifically prohibited to them, and several sets of courts of limited jurisdiction, which can hear only those types of actions specifically <u>consigned</u> to them. 위임하다, 회부하다, 맡기다

2. Exclusive Versus Concurrent Jurisdiction

A great number of cases **can be heard only in state courts**. For some other cases, the federal and state courts have <u>concurrent</u> jurisdiction. A few types of cases are restricted by federal statute to the exclusive jurisdiction of the federal courts. 공동의, 경합하는

<u>II. Federal Courts</u>

The federal judicial power is regulated by Article III, Section 2 of the U.S. Constitution.

Article III of the Federal Constitution <u>establishes</u> the Supreme Court, and Articles I and III **give Congress the power to establish lower federal courts**. The result is a number of federal courts, including the basic pyramid of 94 district courts, 13 courts of appeals, and the Supreme Court. These federal courts are **courts of limited jurisdiction**. Accordingly, for a case to come within the jurisdiction of a federal court, the case normally must fall (1) within a federal statute <u>bestowing</u> jurisdiction on the court and 설립하다 주다, 수여하다

(2) within the outer bounds of federal jurisdiction marked by Article III and the Eleventh Amendment.

1. Federal Question Jurisdiction

As the most important example of federal subject-matter jurisdiction, the district courts have original jurisdiction over cases arising under the Constitution, federal statutory or common law, or treaties. This can be derived from 28 U.S.C. 1331, which Congress has enacted.

There is no precise definition of a case "arising under" the Constitution or laws of the United States. But in the vast majority of cases, the reason there is a federal question is that federal law is the source of the plaintiff's claim.

큰, 거대한

원천, 근거

a) Interpretation of Federal Law

It is not enough that the plaintiff is asserting a state-created claim which requires **interpretation of federal law**.

b) Claim Based on the Merits

If the plaintiff's claim clearly "arises" under federal law, it qualifies for federal question jurisdiction even if the claim is invalid on the merits. Here, the federal court must dismiss for failure to state a claim upon which relief may be granted

c) Anticipation of Defense

The federal question must be integral to plaintiff's cause of action, as revealed by plaintiff's complaint. It does not suffice for federal question jurisdiction that plaintiff anticipates a defense based on a federal statute, or even that defendant's answer does in fact raise a federal question. Thus the federal question must be part of a "well pleaded complaint."

공개하다 / 충족하다

2. Diversity of Citizenship

For another example, the district courts have original jurisdiction over cases that are between parties of **diverse citizenship** and that satisfy a jurisdictional amount requirement (U.S.C. 28 §1332(a)(1)-(4)).

a) Date For Determining

The existence of diversity is determined as of the commencement of the action. If diversity existed between the parties on that date, it is not defeated because one of the parties later moved to a state that is the home state of the opponent.

시작

b) Domicile

What controls for citizenship is domicile, not residence. A person's domicile is where she has her true, fixed and permanent home.

aa) Resident Alien

A **resident alien** (an alien who lives in the United States permanently) is deemed a citizen of the state in which he is domiciled.

bb) Presence of Foreigner

In a suit between citizens of different states, the fact that a foreign citizen (or foreign country) is a party does not destroy diversity.

c) Complete Diversity

The single most important principle to remember in connection with diversity jurisdiction is that "complete diversity" is required. That is, it must be the case that no plaintiff is a citizen of the same state as any defendant.

d) Amount in Controversy

It is also important to note that diversity jurisdiction only applies if the amount in controversy exceeds the sum of U.S.$ 75000 exclusive of costs and interests (28 U.S.C. §1332(b)).

초과하다
이자

e) Pleading not Dispositive

In order to determine whether diversity exists, the pleadings do not settle the question of who are adverse parties. Instead, the court looks beyond the pleadings, and arranges the parties according to their real interests in the litigation.

III. Supplemental Jurisdiction

The courts generally read the Constitution and the jurisdictional statutes to permit the district courts when desirable to hear state claims that were related to pending federal claims. Now Congress has codified this doctrine in 28 U.S.C. § 1367.

소송 계속중인

D. Venue

Venue refers to the **place within a sovereign jurisdiction in which a given action is to be brought**. It matters only if jurisdiction over the parties has been established.

I. State action

In state trials, venue is determined by statute. The states are free to set up virtually any venue rules they wish, without worrying about the federal constitution.

1. Residence

Most commonly, venue is authorized based on the county or city where the defendant resides. Many states also allow venue based on where the cause of action arose, where the defendant does business. 군(郡)

2. Forum non conveniens

Under the doctrine of forum non conveniens, **the state may use its discretion not to hear the case in a county where there is statutory venue**. Sometimes, this involves shifting the case to a different place within the state. At other times, it involves the state not having the case take place in-state at all. Usually, it is the defendant who moves to have the case dismissed or transferred for forum non conveniens. 재량

II. Venue in Federal Actions

In federal actions, the venue question is, "Which federal district court shall try the action? Venue is controlled by 28 U.S.C. §1391. 심리하다, 다루다

1. Three methods

There are three basic ways by which there might be venue in a particular judicial district:

- if any **defendant resides in that district**, and all

defendants reside in the state containing that district;
- ▸ if a "**substantial part of the events**... giving rise to the claim occurred, or a substantial part of property that is the subject of the action is situated," **in the district**; and 발생하다
- ▸ if at least one **defendant is "reachable" in the district**, and no other district qualifies.

2. "Defendant's residence" venue

For both diversity and federal question cases, venue lies in any district where any defendant resides, so long as, if there is more than one defendant, all the defendants reside in the state containing that district.

3. "Place of events or property" venue

For both diversity and federal question cases, venue lies in any district "in which a substantial part of the events or omissions giving rise to the claim occurred, or a substantial part of property that is the subject of the action is situated...." This is "place of events" venue.

4. No "plaintiff's residence" venue

There is no venue (as there used to be) based on plaintiff's residence.

5. Corporation

The residence of a corporation for venue purposes matters only if the corporation is a defendant. A corporation is deemed to be a resident of any district as to which the corporation would have the "minimum contacts" necessary to support personal jurisdiction if that district were a separate state. Thus a corporation is a resident of at least the district where it has its principal place of business, any district where it has substantial operations, and probably any district in its state of incorporation. But merely because a corporation does business somewhere in the state, this does not make it a resident of all districts of that state. 간주하다(hier : 간주되는)

Diagram 26

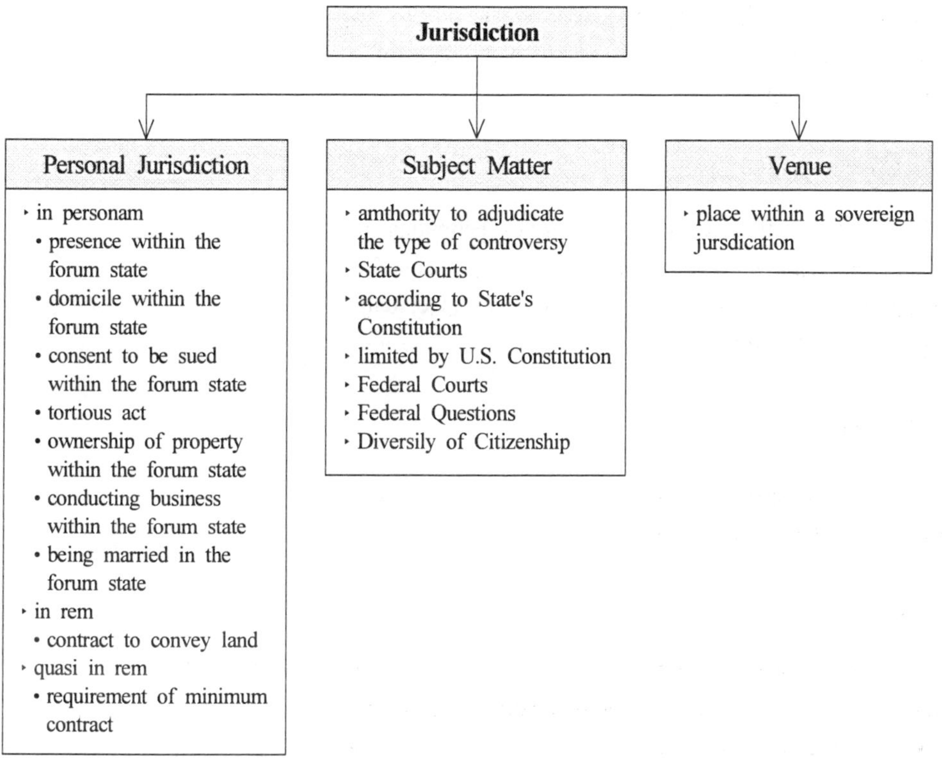

Part 5: Class Action

A. Introduction

The class action is a procedure whereby a single person or small group of co-parties may represent a larger group, or "class," of **persons sharing a common interest**. 대표하다

I. Jurisdiction

In the class action, only the representatives must satisfy the requirements of personal jurisdiction, subject-matter jurisdiction, and venue.

II. Binding on absentees

The results of a class action are generally binding on the

absent members. Therefore, all kinds of procedural rules exist to make sure that these absentees receive due process (e.g., they must receive notice of the action, and notice of any proposed settlement). 부재자

III. Defendant class

In federal practice, as well as in states permitting class actions, the class may be composed either of plaintiffs or defendants. The vast majority of the time, the class will be composed of plaintiffs.

B. Prerequisites

Here are the three prerequisites which must be met before any federal class action is allowed:

I. Size

The class must be so large that joinder of all members is impractical. Nearly all **class actions involve a class of at least 25 members**, and most involve substantially more (potentially tens of thousands). The more geographically dispersed the claimants are, the fewer are needed to satisfy the size requirement. 소의 병합 퍼뜨리다(hier : 퍼져있는)

II. Typical claims

The claims or defenses of the representatives must be "typical" of those of the class. This requirement of "typicality" is also rarely a problem.

III. Fair representation

Finally, the representatives must show that they can "fairly and adequately protect the interests of the class." Thus the **representatives must not have any conflict of interest with the absent class members**, and they must furnish competent legal counsel to fight the suit.

C. Binding effect

Judgment in a class action is binding, whether it is for or against the class, on all those whom the court finds to be members of the class.

A person may **opt out, i.e., exclude himself, from the action**, by notifying the court to that effect prior to a date specified in the notice of the action sent to him. A person who opts out of the action will not be bound by an adverse judgment, but conversely may not assert collateral estoppel to take advantage of a judgment favorable to the class.

불리한

D. Attorneys' fees

The court may award **reasonable attorneys fees to the lawyers for the class**. These fees are generally in rough proportion to the size of the recovery on behalf of the class.

I. Federal statute requires

In the usual case of a class action brought under a federal statute, attorneys fees may be awarded only if a federal statute so provides. Congress has authorized attorneys fees for many important federal statutes that are frequently the subject of class action suits (e.g., civil rights and securities law).

Further reading

Crump e.a., Cases and Materials on Civil Procedure (4th ed., 2001); *Simon*, The Anatomy of a Lawsuit (1996); *Shreve/Raven-Hansen*, Understanding Civil Procedure (2nd ed., 1994); *Kane/Miller*, Civil Procedure (1993); *Green*, Basic Civil Procedure (1979); *Moore*, Federal Practice (looseleaf).

Vocabulary

【 A 】

abolish 폐지하다
abortion 낙태
access 접근(권)
according ~에 따라, ~에 의하여
account 구좌
accounting 회계, 계산, 부기
acknowledge 인정하다, 승인하다
acquittal 무죄방면, (채무의) 변제
act 법률, 법령
action 소송
actionable 소송으로 청구가능한
adjudicate 판결을 내리다
admit (입학을) 허가하다, 인정하다
admission 입학허가, 인정
advice 자문
affidavit 선서, 선서진술서
affirm 확인하다
agency 대리
agent 대리인
agreement 계약, 합의
allegation 주장
ambassador 대사
amendment 수정조항, 수정안, 수정
annual 한해의
anti-trust 반독점
appeal 항소, 상고, 상소
appellate 항소의, 상고의, 상소심의
apply 적용하다, 신청하다
application 신청, 지원
appoint 임명하다
arbitration 중재
argument 논증
arraignment 법정에 소환하여 죄의 인정 여부를 심문함, 죄상 인부(認否)
articles of incorporation 회사설립계약서, 정관
assault 폭행
assent 동의
asset 재산, 자산
assignment 배당, 위임
association 협회, 회사, 연합체
attorney 변호사
authority 권능, 권한, 대리권

【 B 】

bail 보증금, 담보, 보증, 보석금, 보석
ballot 선거
bancrupt 파산의, 지불능력이 없는
bancruptcy 파산
bar 막다, 방해하다, 변호사(전체)
bargain 거래
battery 신체상해
bench trial 배심원없는 법정절차
benefit 이용하다, 이익, 유용함
BFP(Bona Fide Purchaser) 선의취득자
bill 법안
board of directors (주식회사의) 이사회
branch 지점, 지사
brief 소장
burden of proof 입증책임
business 사업, 사업체
bylaw 정관

【 C 】

cancel 취소하다
candidate 후보, 응시자, 지원자
canvass 선거운동을 하다, 유세하다
capable ~할 수 있는
capacity 능력
capital 재산, 자본
case 사례, 경우
cause ~하게끔 하다, 원인을 제공하다
certificate 증명서
certify 증명하다
certiorari denied 상소 기각

chairman 의장
charitable corporation 공익성의 (사단)법인
Chief Justice 미국연방 대법원장
civil 시민의, 시민사회의
claim 주장하다, 청구하다
classify 분류하다
client 의뢰인
closed corporation 소수의 사원으로 구성된 물적 결합회사(유한회사와 유사함)
codify 법제화하다
collateral 부수의, 이면(계약)
collective 공동의, 집단의
collusion 비밀의 합의, 담합
Commerce 무역부
commercial 무역의
commission 위원회
common law 커먼로, 불문법(不文法)
company 회사
compensation 배상, 정당한 보상
compensatory damages 보충적 성격의 손해배상
complaint 제소, 소를 제기함
compulsory 강제의
conduct 태도, 행위
confirm 확인해주다
conflict of laws 법의 충돌, 국제사법
congress 의회
consent 동의
consideration 반대급부, 댓가
constitution 헌법
construe 해석하다
contract 계약
contributory negligence 공동(과실)책임
co-ownership 공동소유(권)
corporate 회사
corporation 물적결합회사, 물적회사
counterclaim 반소
covenant 계약, 날인증서, 계약조항
creditor 채권자
culpable 유책한

D

damage 손해
deceptive 속이는
defamation 중상모략
defect 하자
defendant 피고
defense 국방
demurrer 항변, 이의
denial 부정, 부인
deposition (법정 밖에서 행한) 선서진술서
detriment 불이익, 손해
director 책임자
disclaimer 거절, 거부, 포기
discovery 발견, 공개
discretion 재량
dismiss 기각하다
donation 기부, 기증, 증여
draft 초안
due 의무가 있는, 지불기가 도래한
duress 강제
duty 의무

E

easement 지역권(地役權)
effective date 발효일
election 선거
employ 고용하다
employee 근로자
employer 고용주
enact 법률을 제정하다
encumbrance (저당권 등의) 부담
enforcement 강제, 관철(소송으로 권리를 관철하는 일)
equity 형평법
establish (법률을) 제정하다, (역할을) 확립하다, 수립하다
estate 유산, 재산
estoppel 금반언
evidence 증거
excess 과도한, 남은
executive 행정
exemplary damages 징계적(↔ 보충적) 의미의 손해배상
expiration 소멸
extrinsic evidence (문서로부터 직접 알 수 없는) 외부의 증거

F

fact 사실(관계)
fact-finding 사실관계의 확정
false 틀린
fault (과실 등의) 책임

federal 연방의
federation 연방
fee 수수료
felony 범죄
fiction of law 법적 추정
fiduciary 신탁인
file 제출하다, 서류철
filing 제출, 문서분류
fine (형)벌
firm 회사
first instance(court of first instance) 1심
fixture 설치물
force 권능
foreclose 강제집행하게 하다
foreclosure 강제집행
foreseeability 예측가능성
forfeit 권리를 상실하다, 실권하다
forum 재판관할, 법정
fraud 사기, 속임, 부정수단
fraudulent 사기적인
fund 자금을 대다
fundamental 근본적인

G

gift 선물, 증여
going concern 이익을 남기는 일 또는 기업
good faith 선의
goods 상품, 재화
goodwill 회사의 명성, 좋은 평판
govern 통치하다
government 정부
grand jury 대배심, 기소배심
grant 증서로서 양도하다
gross 총(總), 큰
gross negligence 큰 과실
guarantee 담보, 보증
guarantor 보증인
guidelines 지침
guilty 유책한

H

habitual 습관적인
hand over 양도하다, 이전하다
headquarters 본사, 센터
hearing 변론, 구두심리
hearsay evidence 전문(傳聞) 증거
holder 점유자
hot pursuit 추격권

I

identify 동일함을 확인하다, 식별하다
identity 정체성, 동일성, 주체성
i.e. 즉, 다시말해
illegal 불법의
illegitimate 부적법한, 허락되지 않는, 적출이 아닌
illicit 금지하다
immovable 부동의
immovables 부동산
impeach 탄핵하다
impeachment 탄핵
implied 암시된
import 수입
impose 부과하다
impossibility of performance 이행불능, 급부불능
income 수입
incompetent 무능한
incorporate (자본회사를) 설립하다
incorporation 회사설립
increase 증가
indebted 빚을 진
indefeasible right 불가침의 권리
indict 기소하다, 고발하다
indictment 기소장, 공소문
indorse 보증하다, 배서하다
inevitable 불가피한
infringement 침해
inherit 상속하다
injunction (중지)가처분
injure 침해하다, 위반하다
injustice 부정의
innocent 책임없는
insane 정신이상의
insolvency 지불불능
inspection 조사
instance 경우, 심급
instrument 증서
insult 욕하다
insurance 보험
intent 의도
interest 이자, 이해관계
Internal Revenue Service(IRS) 미국의 재무관청

intimidate 겁주다, 협박하다
intrinsic evidence (문서에서 도출한) 내부적 증거
invasion of privacy 프라이버시 침해
invoice 청구서
issue (규정을) 발하다, 제정하다, 문제, 쟁점
item 항목, 대상

[J]

joinder 소의 병합, 공동소송
joint 연합, 공동의
joint and several 공동채무자적인
joint tenancy 합유적(합수적) 소유권
judge 판사
judgement 판결
judicature 사법제도
judicial 판사의, 법원의
judiciary 사법부, 사법제도
jurisdiction 관할권
juror 배심원, 참심원
jury 배심원
justice 정의
justify 정당화하다

[K]

know-how 노하우
knowingly 고의적으로
knowledge 지식

[L]

Labor 노동부
laches 권리상실, 실권, 권리의 해태, 유책한 지체
lack 부족, 흠결
land 토지
landlord 임대인, 지주
landowner 토지소유자
lapse of time 시간, 시간의 경과
late 늦은
law 법
lawful 적법한
law-making 입법
lawsuit 소송
lawyer 변호사
layman 비전문가
lease 임대계약
leasing 리징
legal 합법적
legislate 법률을 제정하다
legislation 입법
legislature 입법부
lender 채권자
lessee 임차인
lessor 임대인
levy (세금) 징수
liability 책임(즉, 배상의무 등)
liable 책임을 지는
libel 명예손상
liberty 자유
license 라이센스, 허락
likelihood 개연성
limit 한계
limited liability 유한책임
limited liability company 유한(책임)회사
limited partnership 합자회사
litigate 소송하다
litigation 소송
loan 대출
lose 잃다, 지다
loss 손실

[M]

machinery 기계류
mail 우편
maintenance 유지
majority 다수
malice 고의
malicious 악의의
malpractice (의사의) 오진, 오시술
mandate 대리권, 위임
mandatory 의무적인
mark 기호, 표식
matter 문제, 사안
measure 계량, 계측
mediate 중재하다
membership 회원권
mental(ly) 정신적(으로)
mercantile law 상법
merchantable quality 상거래에 일반적인 품질
merge 합병하다
merits of the case 소의 청구이유
Michaelmas 9월 29일, 가을회기

minority 소수
micarriage of justice 사법착오
misconduct 위법행위, 공직의무위반
misdemeanour 범법행위
misuse 남용
mitigation 경감, 축소
mortgage 저당권
motion 청구
motion to dismiss 기각청구
move 움직이다
movables 동산
municipal 도시의, 지방자치단체
municipality 시행정
mutual 상호간의

【N】

naturalization 귀화
necessaries 필요품
necessity (생존) 필수품
neglegt 태만하다, 경시하다
negligence 과실
negligent 과실의
negotiate 흥정하다, 협상하다
negotiation 협상
net 순(純)
nominal 명목상의, 중요하지 않은
nominal damages 경미한 손해배상
nomiate 지명하다
nominee 후보
non-profit corporation 비영리사단
notary public 공증인
note 통지
nuissance 약을 올림, 골탕
null and void 무효

【O】

oath 선서
obey 준수하다
obedience 복종
obiter dicta 부차적인 판결사유
object 목적, 대상, 목표
obligate 의무를 지우다
obligation 의무
obsolete 낡은, 진부한
obtain 얻다
occupier 주민, 거주민
offer 청약
offeree 청약의 수령자
offeror 청약자
office 사무실
official 공적인, 공무의
omit ~을 빠트리다, 누락하다
omission 누락, 생략
operating 가동, 운영
operating budget 운영예산
operation 사업, 활동
opinion 의견, 결정
opponent 상대
oppose 거절하다, 반대하다
option 옵션
oral 구두의
order 위임, 위탁, 요구
ordinance 지방법
origin 기원
originate 발생하다
outcome 결과
outline 초안, 개관
out of court 법정 밖에서, 재판외의
overrule 폐지하다
own 소유하다
owner 소유권자
ownership 소유권

【P】

panel 배심원, 패널
papers 문서
paragraph 조문
paralegal 변호사 사무보조인
parliament 의회
parol 구두(계약)
parol evidence 구두 증거
partial 부분적
partner 지분권자
partnership 인적회사
patent 특허
patented 특허를 받은
patentee 특허권자
pawn 저당물, 질권
pawnbroker 질권자, 전당포업자
pay 지불하다
payable 지불기가 도래한
paycheck 봉급수표
payee 지불의 수령자

payer 지불자
payment 지불
peace 공공질서
pecuniary 돈의, 금전상의
penalty 벌
pending 소송계속중인
pending action ~ 소송
pension 연금
perform 수행하다
performance 이행
peril 위험
period 기간
perjury 위증(죄)
permission 허가
(in) perpetuity 영원히
personal 개인적으로, 직접
personal assets 유동적 사유재산
personal income 개인적 수입
personal injury (신체)상해
personal services 인적 서비스, 용역
petition 청원, 청구
petitioner 신청인, 원고, 청원자
plaint 소
plaintiff 원고
plant 공장
plead 방어하다, 변론하다
pleadings 변론
pledge 담보물
pledgee (동산) 질권자, 저당권자
pledger 질권설정자, 담보잡히는 사람
policy 정책, 원칙
poll 투표
popular 인기있는
possess 소유하다, 점유하다
possession 소유, 점유
possessory 점유권적인
postpone 미루다
power 권능
preamble 전문
precedent 선례, 선판례
preclude 배제하다
predecessor 전임자
preferred stock 우선주
pregnancy 임신
preliminary 명확성
premises 전제
presidency 대통령 재직
presume 전제하다
presumption 전제
prima facie 일견(一見) cf) a ~ case
privacy 사생활, 프라이버시
privilege 특권
privileged documents (법적 소추에서 제외된) 특권적 문서
probative 증거력이 강한
procedure 절차
(legal) proceedings 재판절차
proceeds 수입, 판매액
profession 직업
profit 이익
progress 진보
prohibit 금지하다
prohibition 금지
promise 약속, 청약의 조건
promisee 약속을 받는 자
promisor (의무이행의) 약속을 하는 자
promissory estoppel 약속의 금반언, 약속을 행하여서 발생한 표견(表見)책임
promote 진흥, 촉진하다
proof 증거
property 물권법, 소유권
proposal 제안
proprietor 소유권자
prosecution 형사소추
protection 보호
prove 증명하다
provision 규정, 조항
proxy vote 대리인을 통해 행사한 표
public 공공의
public policy 공공정책, 공공의 이해
publish 출판공개하다
Punitive damages 형벌적 손해배상
purchase 구매하다
purchaser 구매자
pursuant to ~에 따라, ~에 의거하여
pursuit 목적, 추구사항

Q

qualify ~할 권한을 부여하다
quarterly 분기당
questioning 심문, 질문함
quit 그만두다

[R]

race 인종
rate 요금, 비율
real property 부동산
realty 부동산
reasoning 논증, 논거
receive 수령하다, 부여받다.
receivables 채권
reciprocal 호혜적인, 상반하는
reciprocity 쌍무관계, 상반관계, 호혜관계
recognize 인식하다, 알아채다
recommendation 추천
redeem 값을 치르다, 구속하다
referee 중재판사, 심판
register 등록부, 등기부
register of companies 상업등기부, 회사 등기부
register of shareholders 주주등기부
relief 구제책, 원조
remedy (법률적) 구제책
rent 임대료
reserve 보류하다, 유보하다
residence 체류지
resident 주민
resign 사임하다, 해약하다
respondeat superior 수임인에 대한 위임인의 불법행위책임
restrain order 가처분명령
review (재)검토하다
revoke 철회하다
revocation 철회
right 권리, 청구권
rule 규칙
rule of law 법치주의

[S]

sack 해고하다
safety 안전
sale 판매
sample 표본
schedule 계획
scope 범위, 범주
seal 도장, 직인
search 수색
search warrant 수색영장
secret 비밀의
Secretary of State 미국 외무부(국무부) 장관
Secretary of the Interior 내무부 장관
Secretary of the Treasury 재무부 장관
securities 유가증권
segregation 인종분리
self-defence 정당방어, 자기방어
seller 판매자, 매도인
Senate 상원
sentence 벌
separation of powers 권력분립
service 용역, 서비스
servient tenement 편익을 제공하는 토지, 승역지(承役地)
severance 공동점유의 해소, 공동소유관계의 해소
share 공유하다
shareholder 주주
shipment 선적
shipping 선적
signatory 서명자
sitting 법원의 구두재판, 변론
slander 명예훼손, 중상
sole proprietor 단독소유권자
solvent 지불능력이 있는
sovereignty 주권
specimen 표본
spouse 배우자
stare decisis "뻣뻣한 판결"
State Department 외부부(국무부)
statute 법률
statute-barred 시효가 지난
Statute of Limitations 시효에 관한 절차법
stock 재고
Stock Exchange 주식시장
subpoena 강제
subsidiary company 자회사
subsidy 보조금
substantial 중요한, 본질적인
sue 소로써 청구하다, 제소하다
sufferance 묵인, 용인
suit 소
summary judgment 신속절차의 판결

[T]

tangible 손으로 만질 수 있는, 유형의
tariff 관세, 관세표

tax 세금, 조세
tax-exempt 면세의
tenancy 임대계약관계
tenant 세입자
term 개념
terminate 끝내다
testify 증언하다
total 총(總)
trade 무역
trademarks 상표
trader 상인
trade union (영) 노조, (미) labor union
transcript 사본, 의사록
treaty 조약
trespass 주거침입, 불법침입
trespass to chattels 소유권 행사의 방해
trespasser 주거침입자, 불법침입자
trial 재판
trust 신탁
trustee 수탁자

【 U 】

ultra vires 월권행위
unanimous 한 목소리로
unavoidable 불가피한
unconstitutional 위헌의
unilateral 일방적
unincoporated association 미등기사단, 권리능력없는 사단
union 연합체
unjust 부당한, 불공평한
unjust enrichment 부당이익
unlimited 무제한의
unliquidated damages 미확정 손해배상청구권
unpaid 지불되지 않은
unreasonable 과도한
unsecured creditor 담보를 확보하지 않은 채권자
usage 관습, 관행
use 사용하다
usual 보통의
usurp 빼앗다, 강탈하다

【 V 】

vacant 비어있는, 미점유의
valid 유효한
validat 유효한 것으로 선언하다
validity 유효성
valuable 가치있는
valuables 귀중품(보석류)
value 가치
value added tax(VAT) 부가가치세
vendee 매수인
vendor 매도인
venue 관할법원
verbal 구두의
verdict 배심원의 평결
verify 입증하다, 증명하다
versus(v.) 대(對)
vest 부여하다, 점유를 이전하다
vested interest (미래의 점유권에 대한) 확정된 권리
vested remainer 불가침의 기대권
veto 거부권을 행사하다
vicarious 간접적인, 대리인을 통한
vice 부(副)
violate 침해하다
void 무효의, 법적 구속력이 없는
voidable 취소가능한
voluntary 자발적인
vote 투표
voter 투표권자
vouch for ~를 위하여 보증하다
voucher 보증인, 상품권

【 W 】

waive (권리 등을)포기하다
waiver 포기
warranty 보증
welfare 복지
whereas ~을 살펴보건대(계약서의 前文에서 사용하는 상투어)
wholesale 도매업
willful 고의의
wind up a company 회사를 청산하다
withdraw 철회하다, (소송을) 취하하다, 취소하다
withhold 보류하다
witness 증인
writ 법원의 문서, 처분, 결정
writ of certiorari 상소를 허락하는 법원의 결정
wrongful 불법적인

Index

편저자 : **조익제**

독일 최대의 지식재산권 전문로펌 Bardehle & Partner(뮌헨)에서 3년간 근무하는 동안, 독일 및 미국 의뢰인을 대리하여 상담과 송무를 진행하였다. 2005년 귀국이후 현재까지 Lee International IP&Law Group(서울)에서 외국 변호사로 근무하고 있다. 국내유일의 미국 로스쿨인 한동국제법률대학원에서 비교특허법 등을 강의하였으며, 성균관대학교 법과대학원에서 박사과정을 수료하였다. 비교법적인 차원에서 영미법에 큰 관심을 가지고 있으며, 함께 배워가는 마음으로 영미법 시리즈를 편집하여 소개하고 있다.

EADS의 Euro-Fighter 전투기 관련 특허침해소송, Siemens 상표분쟁 및 의약품 관련 국제 손해배상소송에서 Celltech 등의 다국적 기업을 성공적으로 대리하였다.

기타 저서
- 표준 라이센스 계약(한-영판, 792쪽), 2004, 공저(파겐베르크, 가이슬러, 조익제)
- Leitfaden zum Koreanischen Patentrecht (독일어판, 한국특허법 매뉴얼), 2006

근무처
www.leeinternational.com, icho@leeinternational.com

조익제 변호사와 함께 영어로 읽는

미국법 입문(2)

Introduction to the US American Legal System

for Korean Speaking Lawyers and Law Students

2004년 12월 1일 초판 발행
2009년 3월 1일 재판 발행

편저자 조 익 제
발행인 고 준 영
발행처 **법 영 사**

(135-280) 서울시 강남구 대치동 611
전화 (501) 8898(대) FAX (501) 8895
등록 1987.11.5 제3-125호(윤)
Homepage : www.bubyoungsa.co.kr
E-mail : bypuco@chollian.net

정가 **15,000원**

※ 저자와의 협의에 의하여 인지첨부를 생략함.
※ 본서는 ALPMANN SCHMIDT사와 본사와의 특약에 의해 독점 출판되었습니다.

ISBN 978-89-7032-254-4

조익제 변호사와 함께 영어로 읽는
「영국민사법 입문」, 「미국법 입문」 시리즈 안내

◀ **조익제 변호사와 함께 영어로 읽는** 「영국 민사법 입문 Vol. 1」

2008.2.1 초판발행 / 4·6배판 / 252면 / 값 15,000원

「영국민사법 입문」 제1권은 주로 **영국법 개론**과 **계약법**을 상세히 다루고 있다. 미국법의 기초를 이루는 **Common Law 제도**는 과연 무엇인가? 미국법의 깊은 이해를 위해서는 **영미법 전반에 대한 이해**가 필수적이며, 이런 의미에서 본서는 미국법 입문 중 **계약법 내용을 심화**하고 있다. 본서의 **생동감 있는 판례 소개**와 서술방식, 다양한 도표들은 법이란 무엇인가 하는 질문을 매우 구체적으로 답변해 준다.

조익제 변호사와 함께 영어로 읽는 「영국 민사법 입문 Vol. 2」 ▶

「영국민사법 입문」 제2권은 민사법의 전통적인 분류인 **불법행위법, 재산법, 신탁법, 친족법** 그리고 **상속법**을 강의하고 있다. 영미법체계를 지닌 나라의 문화와 제도를 이해하기 위해서는 그 바탕이 되는 제도를 잘 이해하여야 한다. 일상적인 정보를 넘어서서, **영미법 국가의 고급 정보**를 소화하기 위해서는 그 나라의 다양한 법을 잘 파악하고 있어야 한다. 전문적인 법률정보를 찾아 이해하려고 하는 사람의 경우에는 말할 것도 없다. 본 시리즈의 독서를 마친 뒤에는 새로운 지평에서, 미국을 포함한 영미법 세계로부터의 정보를 접할 수 있을 것이다. <근간>

◀ **조익제 변호사와 함께 영어로 읽는** 「미국법 입문 Vol. 1」

2006.4.1 재판발행 / 4·6배판 / 232면 / 값 15,000원

「미국법 입문」 제1권은 **헌법과 계약법**을 상세히 설명하고 있다. 법학 전반에 관심을 가진 **모두가 읽을 수 있는 책**이며, 잘 요약된 **미국의 판례를 직접 읽는 즐거움**을 준다. 한글 설명은 사전을 대체할 수도 없고, 대체해서도 안되지만, 단어 때문에 독서가 방해되는 일을 방지하여, 영어독서 그 자체의 묘미를 가지게 해줄 것이다. 미국법에 관한 원서독서는 한국법을 바라보는 새로운 시각을 갖게 해줄 것이다.

표준 라이센스 계약
License Agreements

▶ 변호사, 파겐베르크 / 가이슬러 / 조익제 공저 / 2005. 2. 15 초판발행 / 크라운판 / 822면 / 값 39,000원 ◀

본서는 기술이전과 관련한 14개의 표준적인 계약서를 제시하며, 그와 관련된 법적인 논점들을 상세히 해설하고 있다.

본서의 유럽판은 실무계의 필요와 학문적인 깊이를 함께 고려하여 양쪽의 인정을 고르게 받아온 권위서이며, 베스트 셀러이다.

본서는 영한대역의 형식을 취하고 있다. 따라서 외국인들과의 협상에 필요한 용어들을 미리 익힐 수 있는 장점도 있다.

본서는 한국의 상황을 반영하는 추가의 주석을 통해, 우리의 현실에도 적합한 책이다.